T0197321

This book is dedicated to the 4 most important women in my life:

To my daughter Rebecca, who is a constant joy and makes me proud to be her Dad,

To my sister Vera, who keeps me honest and never lets me get too big headed,

To my life partner Shayla, who lovingly helps edit my writing and my life and

To my niece Anna, The California girl who will probably turn out be a better writer than I ever will.

UnCommon Sense
Unusual Lessons from the Workplace

Dr. Tom Steiner
The EnterTRAINer
October, 2016

authorHOUSE®

AuthorHouse™
1663 Liberty Drive
Bloomington, IN 47403
www.authorhouse.com
Phone: 1 (800) 839-8640

Published by AuthorHouse 11/07/2016

ISBN: 978-1-5246-4779-7 (sc)
ISBN: 978-1-5246-4777-3 (hc)
ISBN: 978-1-5246-4778-0 (e)

Library of Congress Control Number: 2016917999

Contents

CHANGE

A FEW MORE IDEAS THAT NO ONE TALKS ABOUT

GETTING STARTED

CHAPTER 1

WHAT IS UNCOMMON SENSE?

If you spend enough time in the business world, you will meet leaders with all different kinds of smarts. Book smarts. Street smarts. Emotional smarts. Smarts that come from years of real world experience. Some people rely heavily on just one category of smarts. Others put all of their smarts together and simply call it "Common Sense."

This book isn't about having "Common Sense." Common Sense is no longer enough to succeed today. Instead, today's world has become increasingly an era characterized by "UnCommon Sense."

What is "UnCommon Sense? UnCommon Sense requires that you put together everything that you have learned with three other components:

1) Heart (care, compassion and concern),
2) Emotional Sensitivity and Guts (intuition and the ability to "thin slice" situations coupled with the willingness to pull the trigger and leap into action) and
3) Courage (a good sense of when to stretch and/or break rules and when to set new precedents by using disruptive thinking).

Before I offer you numerous examples of UnCommon Sense, I want to honor time tested elements of Common Sense. There is a lot to be said for Common Sense. Let me offer you Dr. Tom's Top 5 Bits of Wisdom that I have learned from books, in the street, as a psychologist, coach and counselor, and from the school of hard knocks.

BOOK SMARTS

1) Numbers don't lie. Particularly the bottom line. Thoughts, dreams, wishes and hopes are all terrific, but at the end of the month you have to pay salaries and rent. Money talks. Everything else walks.
2) If you can't measure it, you can't manage it. Know the right metrics. Have the right processes in place. Look at them frequently and be agile and ready to adjust to changing situations in the ever- changing world.
3) Find out what the world wants and then find a way to sell it to them at the right time in the right place in the right way. Some businesses don't check in often enough with their customers and potential customers to make sure that they have the right product at the right price, a product which can be readily available and supported.
4) Get it in writing. Goals. Contracts. Expectations. Boundaries. Limits. Talk is cheap and doesn't stand up as well in court.
5) The new concept du jour is "evidence based." Make sure that you have solid research and experience with new tactics before you put them into action. Review "best-in-class" practices, adjust them to fit your environment and then implement them.

STREET SMARTS

1) Everyone has to have their own unique hustle (be it 3 Card Monte, The Naked Cowboy or The Purple Cow). Make sure you have something unique to offer.
2) The world is not fair. Fair is where pigs win medals. In this world, you get what you take or what you make happen.
3) Play for keeps. There are no do overs. There is no free lunch. If it sounds too good to be true, it probably is too good to be true (particularly if it comes from an unknown Benin official who offers to send you $5Million dollars via email.)
4) The easiest people to "sell" a product or an idea to are greedy people. Those people love to get a "deal." Most salespeople fall into this category.

5) The real value of a product or service is what it costs in the open, unrestricted, street marketplace.

EMOTIONAL SMARTS

1) Feelings matter as much as, if not more than, logic. People buy ideas and products emotionally and then justify their purchases with logic.
2) You usually catch more flies with honey than with vinegar. People like to deal with other people that they like. They also like to deal with other people who they think like them. Be likeable. Like others.
3) It is easy to talk "at" other people. Most people really want to be heard and more importantly to be understood. Communication involves suspending your judgment and becoming curious about what they have to say. What you say matters, BUT how well you listen matters more.
4) Trust and credibility are the 2 factors that drive relationships and businesses. They are the most precious commodities in any relationship. They can only be rebuilt twice in a life time, if damaged.
5) Communication must be intentional, not accidental. It is important to think carefully about everything you say in emails, phone calls and personal meetings. Use "emotionally evocative language." Imagine if you were able to deal with the issues of the day AND plant seeds (of hope or doubt) about the future in every communication. You would be well ahead of the game when it comes time to sell your ideas.

REAL WORLD SMARTS

1) What you did in the past doesn't matter very much. You can't fix yesterday. You can only influence and fix today and tomorrow. You never really own winning. You just rent it. And the rent collector comes every day. Just when you think you can stop running as fast as you can, someone else runs right past you. There is always someone else out there who

may want it more than you do. They are willing and able to work harder than you do if you get complacent. Never relax.

2) No matter how good you are, you can always get better. The best in class are always striving for feedback and continuous improvement. They are always looking over their shoulders to see what is around them. They are willing to borrow, steal or import the ideas of others to make things better. The best companies today import 50% of their ideas from outside the company.

3) Politics are everywhere. There is no such thing as an apolitical situation or organization. However, my definition of politics is different than yours. When I say politics, I don't mean lying, saying yes when you mean no, sugarcoating or kissing up to anyone. Those are old impractical definitions of politics. What I mean by politics is positioning your ideas in front of other people so that they have the maximum ability of being favorably received, while being honest and credible.

4) There are red rules and blue rules. Red rules are engraved in stone and can never be broken. Blue rules are rules that apply most of the time. Most of the business world is blue, not red. The motto for today is "ask for forgiveness, not permission."

5) The world is changing so rapidly that you need to be adept at making changes instantly. The world rewards the first player, the first page and the first respondent. Speed and agility triumph over legacy.

If you have learned all of these things and know how to apply them, you are off to a great start and likely to fit in well in the business world. But if that is all you know, you may top out rather quickly at the level of manager or director. To gain access and have success in the upper echelons of private and public sector organizations requires something additional, something I call UnCommon Sense.

The Difference between Common Sense and UnCommon Sense

How many times have you heard someone say: "That guy may have a lot of degrees and experience, but he has no Common Sense. He couldn't lead his way out of a paper bag." We all have seen leaders who are great at going by the book. Following the rules. Knowing the procedure. Coloring within the lines. But when you chat with them about leading people in a passionate and caring manner, they seem clueless and even worse, disinterested. These leaders assume that their employees will follow their directives and instructions simply because they have to.

Over 500 years ago, Machiavelli told us that "it is better to be feared than loved." Machiavelli may have been correct amidst the carnival of Italian politics of the 1500's, where new leaders were regularly purged and replaced. But he would not be correct today. Too many managers believe that their power lies in their job title. Nothing could be further from the truth. Their real power lies in their ability to work with and motivate a diverse workforce.

Common Sense suggests that leaders should pay primary attention to productivity levels, getting the work done correctly, on time, within budget and up to spec. After that, leaders may be able to afford themselves the luxury of paying attention to their employees' feelings, hopes and aspirations. Lead the tasks and then show your concern for your employees.

UnCommon Sense suggests that you do exactly the opposite. If you show respect, dignity, caring and concern for your employees and lead with passion, it may be easier and more rewarding for you and for them to meet and exceed their work productivity goals.

The UnCommon Sense examples that follow are simple and straight forward. You will be able to put them to use wherever you work, be it in the private sector, public sector or non-profit/charity sector.

Where did I learn UnCommon Sense? From paying attention to everything around me, every single day of my life, in school, at home and in the American workplace.

I have had many jobs. I have worked as a Director of Leadership Development, University Professor and Elementary School Principal. I have also worked as a door-to-door salesperson, taxi cab driver and stand-up comic. I learned UnCommon Sense at every one of those jobs.

I have worked with all kinds of people from white collar to blue collar to no collar. I have worked with "boots on the ground" employees to Senior Level Executives. I have worked and spoken with organizations in 49 of the 50 great states in this country (OK, the 6 esteemed people in South Dakota have not invited me to their state, yet.) I have worked with hotel clerks, bank tellers, truck drivers, dentists, prison guards, nurses, civil servants and engineers. I have learned UnCommon Sense from working with every one of them.

I learned more UnCommon Sense walking into buildings selling cable television and driving cabs in the not so friendly streets of NYC than I ever learned in university classrooms. Sometimes I was treated well. Other times I was treated like a piece of dirt. But UnCommon Sense teaches you that school is always in session, particularly if you are a good student. So pay attention. The school of UnCommon Sense is different from any other school that you have ever attended.

Every job you have will provide new opportunities. Every person you meet can teach you something. Every place you have ever been before, every place you go to now and every place you will ever visit in the future is a place where you can learn something. There is UnCommon Sense everywhere as long as you know where to look for it, are willing to look for it and can understand it.

There are few, if any, textbooks on UnCommon Sense. While you can learn some valuable lessons from reading a book like this, getting out there and putting these ideas into action is the only way to guarantee your success. Life is OJT (on the job training.) Put your "boots on the ground," roll up your shirtsleeves and get ready to jump into the muck and mire.

Much to your dismay, there will be a lot of homework. The world assigns homework every day. The world expects you to practice these lessons and get better and better using them.

There are two differences between homework that you completed at school and this type of homework. First of all, only YOU AND the rest of the world grade your homework, instead of your teacher grading it. You will get graded in terms of your joy, happiness, pay, raises and promotional opportunities. The second difference at this school is that you don't have to do any of your homework to graduate. Everybody graduates. Whether you are ready or not. Whether you are ready to be successful or not. Life is too short not to graduate and go out and find your place in the world. Some people just end up in better places than others.

If you want to make great strides as a leader, pay attention every day to everything you see around you, do your homework and realize that lifelong learning is the name of the game. School never ends for smart people. I got my Ph.D. in 1975. That's over 40 years ago. I got my Management Degree in 1983. We were doing computer programming on punch cards. How much of that education still serves me well today? I'd be a fossil or at least a dinosaur if I didn't work hard to stay current in the school of UnCommon Sense.

The reward for really paying attention and mastering these skills is that you get a bit more freedom and you can work with more interesting and eccentric people and can choose which people to work with and which people to avoid.

In this book, what you will learn is how to work with every kind of human being on the planet in a way that shows caring, builds trust and gets results. Imagine walking into any room of people and believing that you can connect with everyone there, gain commitment, create passion and actually work together effectively and efficiently to accomplish your mutual goals.

In this book Common Sense and UnCommon Sense will be placed side by side for you to look at, think about and evaluate for yourself.

Dr. Tom Steiner

The only way for you to know which is better for you is to try many of the approaches and see which ones result in better outcomes. The more options you try the better. Are you ready?

Let's get started.

CHAPTER 2

MOTIVATING YOUR EMPLOYEES

COMMON SENSE

Employees are motivated by pay, promotional opportunities, perks and time off.

UNCOMMON SENSE

Once employees are making enough money to pay their bills, they are motivated by feeling valued and appreciated. To get peak performance from them involves helping them to feel that they are part of a greater whole and that their work is meaningful to themselves and to others around them.

I often hear leaders say that it is tough to motivate people during a tough economy or in the public sector because there just isn't enough money available to use for pay raises and bonuses. Promotional opportunities are limited to praying for your boss to have a traffic accident in the parking lot. Nonsense.

When I worked as a cabbie, my dispatcher, who made Attila the Hun seem like a saint, doled out the cabs to drivers according to the following factors:

1) What time you showed up for work
2) Whether you brought him food
3) Whether you told him a dirty joke.

So, late, unfunny, foodless drivers always got the worst cabs. They got the cabs that made those noises that led you to believe that you might not get back to the garage at the end of the day. The worst part of it was that he thought that he was a GREAT MOTIVATOR. I was motivated. Motivated to lick any food that I brought him when I was coming down with a cold. I realized early on that I never wanted to treat anyone else that way. No one will work very hard for very long when they feel that their good work has little to do with how they are treated.

Consider these people instead:

Matt works as a busboy in a local restaurant. He has been offered higher paying jobs but has always turned them down. Why? Because he loves working in that restaurant. Everyone knows his name. He looks forward to seeing his regular customers. He enjoys chatting with them. He brings pottery that he has made in his spare time to give to his favorite customers. He knows what is expected of him, and his boss genuinely likes and appreciates him.

Josie is a hygienist in a dental office. This is the 4th different office that she has worked in. She loves it so much at her new office that she gives thanks every day for the opportunity to work there. Is she getting paid more at this office? Maybe a few more dollars. But if you ask her what she really likes, it is the family atmosphere of the office. She feels that she is supported by the doctors, knows her role and is valued by her patients and the rest of the staff.

Think this is true just for service employees? Not so. Life is too short to work just for the money. 90% of chemists working at biotech companies are likely to never work on a drug that actually makes it to the marketplace. Only 1 in 10 will ever experience the satisfaction of knowing that their work directly resulted in developing a treatment that helped folks cope with an illness. Do you see the other 9 people lining up for space on the 9th floor office ledge waiting for their turn to jump off? No. Why not? In many of the better companies, chemists are encouraged to see their work as successful, even if it doesn't result in a saleable drug. Their contribution may have been to rule out other possible formulations and push the research process into another direction. There is no sense of failure. They learn what doesn't work so well.

Think of the people whom you work with. How much appreciation do you show them on a regular basis? I am not talking about the once-a-year company picnic or the insincere "good job," said without any real feelings or specifics attached. I am talking about simple, heartfelt, open communication where you take the time and make the effort to know what they are doing, ask questions about it, think about what they have said and then respond with a unique and meaningful compliment.

Have you taken the time to get every employee to feel like they are part of the bigger picture? There is a classic NASA story about then President Lyndon B. Johnson visiting the NASA Space Center in Houston in the 1960's. He walked up to a janitor and asked the gentleman what his job was. The gentleman beamed back: "Mr. President, my job is to help put a man on the moon." Now that man got it. He saw his role in the grand scheme of things.

THOUGHT BOMBS TO PONDER

1) How many of your employees get it? How many of them see the vision that your organization has? How many of them feel like they are a part of the vision?
2) What are you doing to help them see their part? How can you help your employees develop more connection to their job and the mission?
3) Are you concerned about how your employees feel? Do you ever ask them how they feel? Is their good work linked to their success on the job?
4) Do you take the time to tell your employees how important they are? How often?
5) Do your employees see you as a caring and compassionate leader?

CHAPTER 3

MAKING WORK MEANINGFUL

COMMON SENSE

The amount and quality of work that an employee completes *is what makes a job meaningful.*

UNCOMMON SENSE

Doing a job really well really matters. However, it is the nature of the interactions that employees have with other people WHILE they are doing their job that makes it meaningful to everyone.

Employees who go to work every day without a strong sense of purpose just go to work. They may do high quality work, but at the end of the day, they are tired, worn out and may not leave with a sense of pride and accomplishment.

My goal is simple. I want to help you help your employees COME TO WORK WITH A SMILE ON THEIR FACE AND LEAVE WORK WITH A SMILE ON THEIR FACE 9 OUT OF EVERY 10 DAYS WITH MORE ENERGY THAN THEY HAD WHEN THEY WALKED IN.

There is a good reason for arriving and leaving with a smile on your face. Most people go to work in order to provide for their families. Bringing home enough money to pay for *home, food and other necessities is quite important. However, if you leave all your* energy at work and do not have a lot of emotional energy left for your family when you get home, is it really worth it?

It is important to come home at the end of the day happy. You are more likely to come home happy when you have positive interactions and care about the work you are doing during your day of work.

One of the jobs that I had early in my career was loading UPS trucks at night in the middle of the summer in NYC. Being a non-union temporary worker, I was assigned the least desirable task of stacking boxes and whatever else New Yorkers were shipping that day in the back of a 40-foot-long trailer where the temperature was well over 100 degrees on a regular basis. This was not the most fun I have ever had. My supervisor was not quite the enlightened type. He was as smart as a bag of rocks.

One day after a long week in the back of the truck, I couldn't take it anymore. Hurling packages marked "fragile" against the back of the truck was no longer fun. No one cared whether or not my job was meaningful to me. I felt that I just had to get out of that truck for a while. So, in desperation, I faked a knee injury, claiming that I had twisted my knee, while stumbling over a box.

My supervisor calmly told me that, just for that one day, I could work on the "downloader," making sure that there were no logjams on the conveyor belt. It was still 100 degrees, but at least I was outside of the truck. At the end of night, he asked to see me. I thought he might genuinely be interested in seeing how my knee felt. It felt good to think that I was about to be treated with some compassion.

Instead he took a much more direct tack (as only a true New Yorker could) and told me that, if my leg wasn't better by tomorrow, he would break my other leg. Miraculously my leg healed the very next day. I was promptly sent into the back of the truck again. My body did go back to work, but my mind never returned. I became the classic disgruntled employee complaining about every minor slight. My goal is for you to have "gruntled" employees, employees who care deeply about their jobs.

Needless to say, the only meaning I took from this job was never to ship my parcels using UPS. And certainly not to write the word "fragile" on any of them.

The irony is that participating in the delivery of packaged material can be a meaningful task. After all, you are assisting in the process of bringing valuable goods to other businesses and to individuals. You are part of what keeps Americans productive and happy. Unfortunately, my supervisor never cared that I perceived my job that way.

Consider these people instead:

Henry is a food service worker who serves food every day in a local hospital. He pushes around the same cart carrying various forms and colors of food that he offers to patients 2-3 times a day. All of his patients know Henry and look forward to him showing up in their rooms. Huh? Are these people so hungry and desperate for food that they actually crave the treats that Henry brings? No. It is not the food that matters so much. With Henry, they always get a show with their meal.

One day, Henry comes dancing into your room screaming: "You got the GREEN JELLO today. You lucky dog. Everyone else got red Jell-O, but YOU GOT THE GREEN." The huge smile on his face and the commotion he causes always results in a smile and sometimes applause from his patients. The next day, he comes in with black tooth wax covering his top teeth warning you not to bite into the meat because he broke all of his teeth doing so. Never a dull moment with Henry.

So what is meaningful about his job? Delivering all of his trays on time to the right rooms? No. What Henry most cares about is helping his patients have a better day in the hospital. He has a genuine desire to put a smile on his patient's faces. Patients actually hope that he delivers the wrong tray to their room because the apology is usually done in song.

I learned this same lesson when I used to visit dying patients at our local hospital. One woman taught me a true life lesson. This woman was an inspirational person in our community. Sadie was known everywhere as the kind of person who was always ready to help others and always wanted to bring a smile to your face. After she was diagnosed with cancer, she was given 2 death sentences. The first one came from her doctor who told her that the cancer had spread throughout her body and there wasn't much that could be done to contain or stop it. The worse death sentence came from her family who said: "They didn't want to go into her room and joke with her anymore because they were afraid that IT WOULD UPSET HER."

Of course, they weren't really worried about upsetting her. They were more worried about upsetting themselves. Now in 1978, I had never performed stand-up comedy, but I still fancied myself to be a funny guy. I would walk into her room with arrows through my head or big rabbit ears on and just start chatting. Whenever I walked in with bedpans over my shoes, her face always brightened.

The doctors in the hospital would see me coming down the hall and mutter: "Here comes the fool." One kindly doc pulled me aside and told me that no one would have much respect for me, if I just kept showing up in such silly, unprofessional attire. He ended up lecturing me on maintaining a professional image and keeping professional distance from my clients. I told him that, not only would people respect me, but that I would be their therapist of choice. Not because I was a better therapist than the others, but because I was emotionally genuine and willing to laugh, cry, scream or just sit there according to the patient's desire. Sadie changed my life with one sentence. After a few visits, she said: "You're the only one out there who cares whether I laugh again or not. Everyone else is too busy trying to keep me alive." Wow!

I once did a show at EPCOT (Every Person Comes Out Tired) and happened to come in the back entrance, where employees arrive daily. On the six-story Epcot building, the EPCOT/DISNEY credo of the time was spelled out for all employees to see every day as they came to work. Although there were many great ideas listed on the building, the one that has always stuck with me is:

MAKE SURE EVERY CHILD AND SENIOR CITIZEN HAS A MEMORABLE DAY HERE TODAY.

Why isn't that sentence inscribed on every personal and organizational mission, vision and values statement? Sometimes the smile you bring and the connection between your heart and the hearts of others makes all the difference in the world.

THOUGHT BOMBS TO PONDER

1) Are you encouraging your employees to come to work with this customer-focused attitude this every day? Are they interested in whether or not every customer and every coworker has a memorable day today?

2) How can you help your employees enjoy and appreciate the interactions they have every day with their colleagues and customers? They will go home happier, be more productive and have a true sense of value and meaning most of the time.

3) When was the last time you asked your employees what they felt was important about their job? Do they ever see customer feedback about how the value of the service/ product they provide?

4) Do they see the smile on your face that lets them know that you are enjoying your job?

5) What motto should you have on the door to inspire your employees when they come to work? (When I worked at a Citibank Development Center in Los Angeles, the sign greeting us on the overhead walkway when we entered the building was "The Bank of the Future is Being Created Here Today.)

CHAPTER 4

MOTIVATING THE 5 TYPES OF EMPLOYEES

COMMON SENSE

You can't motivate employees. Employees motivate themselves.

OR

In order to be "fair" to all employees, each employee should be motivated in the same, consistent way.

UNCOMMON SENSE

There are at least 5 different types of employees and each type of employee is driven by a different set of payoffs (benefits) that drive their behavior.

(Note: By the way, the only thing to remember about "fair" is that there are rides there and you get to eat cotton candy. While I am NOT suggesting that you ever be UNFAIR to your employees, treating everyone in the same fashion is more of a de-motivator than a motivator. Democracy is a poor way to run any business.)

Today, leaders have precious little time to spend motivating their employees. Most leadership time is spent attending meetings, dealing with Senior Management, customers and the myriad of record keeping and reporting that seems to be required at work every day. Therefore, every minute invested into employee motivation must be well spent. Each interaction needs to have a very high ROIT. ROIT means Return On Invested Time.

Here is the standard I want you to adopt for every leadership interaction you ever consider implementing. Make sure that for every hour you invest in an employee, you receive back 3-5 hours of increased productivity. That equates to a 300% to a 500% rate of return on your invested time. You should be so lucky to get those types of returns in the financial marketplace. BUT you can and will get those returns and more in the leadership marketplace. Keep that criteria in mind as you read through this and other leadership books and only pick those strategies and tactics that you think will live up to that expectation.

There are 5 basic types of employees in most workplaces. They are:

1) WATER WALKERS

They are your brightest performers. They can do the work that no one else knows how or wants to do. They are eccentrics to the max. Their eccentricities are tolerated because when they are needed, they fly in with the red Superman/Superwoman logo stenciled on their chests with their red capes on their backs and solve the problems du jour. They aren't necessarily well liked by others and they could care less. Most of them could use a healthy dose of "charm school." They are less concerned about results (they rarely count how much they have completed) than they are concerned with doing "challenging work." They may continue to work on something long after it is no longer needed or valued, just because their interest in the work is all consuming.

What motivates Water Walkers?

Don't waste your time or money on raises, plaques or certificates for these folks. That is not the key to motivating Water Walkers. Their payoffs/wants/desires/needs are centered on FREEDOM AND CHALLENGE. The classic test of whether an employee is a Water Walker or not is simple. Just tell this person that Task "A" simply can't be done. They will turn to you and in a true Robert DeNiro (Taxi Driver) moment, simply say: "Are you talking to ME? From that moment on, the task will no longer be referred to as TASK "A" but rather as a "MISSION FROM GOD."

Roger, the top salesperson at the cable television company that I worked for, kept hours that were a tad irregular. He was as talented with a cue stick as he was peddling cable television. Since his afternoons were regularly spent at the local billiard parlor, he only showed up for work on time if:

a) He had won a lot of money;
b) There was no one left to play at the pool hall; OR
c) He had no money left to bet.

Why was this erratic behavior tolerated? Because Roger would turn in sales reports with lots of sales on them every night. Whether he worked for half an hour, 2 hours or 5 hours, Roger never turned in the proverbial "goose egg" (a sales report with zero sales.) While some of Roger's sales were questionable (e.g. Roger might have paid for the customer's first month of CATV out of his own pocket), he always outperformed the pack. Since he was a "solo," no one ever figured out the magic to his performance. Water Walkers rarely ever share their secrets with others. They believe that if "others are not smart enough to figure it out for themselves, then they don't deserve to know."

Butch was a high tech electrical engineer working at a progressive company in San Diego with advanced degrees from MIT. He was also a relatively accomplished surfer. Butch was not the type of employee to keep regular hours at work either. In fact, Butch decided when to come to work more on the basis of the tide tables and surf report. When the surf was good, Butch would work at the beach. When the waves were poorly formed, you would find him at his desk. How many hours did Butch put in weekly? His average work week was close to 60 hours (there was rarely great surf at night.) Why was his behavior tolerated? Because no one else could solve certain problems as fast as Butch could. The bigger the problem, the more engaged Butch was. Butch was not the type of employee who thrived on routine work. Butch thrived working on the problems that everyone else avoided.

Are you interested in developing exceptional performance from exceptional people? Even if they "break a few rules?" Have you provided a work environment that attracts, tolerates and retains these talented eccentrics? From an ROIT standpoint, the average leader doesn't get a huge return on leadership time spent with Water Walkers. That is often the case because that leader doesn't treat these rule benders and breakers in a unique manner. They don't regularly dangle freedom and challenge as the beguiling carrot in front of Water Walkers. The leader becomes increasingly frustrated as the Water Walker refuses to follow the rules, and the Water Walker becomes increasingly alienated and, at worse, walks away.

Instead, think of how you can create challenging opportunities for your most exceptional employees. In the early 1970's, aerospace companies created "skunkworks" inside their companies, where regular work rules were loosened to provide a work climate where aerospace engineers could create the impossible. In the 1980's, when I visited Atari videogames (the video game market leader at the time), I was amazed that every office was covered from floor to ceiling with material to stimulate the minds of the design engineers, software programmers and graphic artists.

Herding cats is not easy. There aren't many cat herders, but the rewards can be tremendous if you are able to become a "cat whisperer."

2) AVERAGE PLUS

They are the work horses on your team. They do the most work. They care about the quality of the work they produce. They keep track of how much they have accomplished. When other people fall behind in their work, that work usually gets reassigned to Average Plus employees. They are the most dependable and team-oriented players. You can recognize them by their "To Do" lists and their orderly desks. They are often admired, well-liked employees who pride themselves on following the "rules." In short, they are the MVP's of your team. Without these people, you might be left dealing only with freaks (Water Walkers) and Under Performers (Average Minus and Human Speed Bumps.)

What motivates Average Plus employees?

Average Plus employees want, deserve and thrive on recognition and appreciation. They also appreciate getting regular raises and bonuses. If you want to show these folks that you care, you should consider strategies that appeal to their heads (new knowledge and training) and to their hearts (recognition in front of their peers and families as well as favorable performance reviews and opportunities for exposure in front of Senior Management). In one sense, these are the easiest people to motivate because they crave recognition and appreciation. While many other employees would cringe at receiving an "Employee of the Month" plaque, Average Plus employees will affix each one of their plaques to the walls in their office.

(Note: If you have been using Employee of the Month or any other motivational promotion for more than 2 years, it may become affectionately known as "Wienie of the Month." After the first deserving candidates get their awards (usually within the first year), the next recipients are more likely to fit under the heading of "at least he is breathing and hasn't lit the office on fire in a while." Consider that most motivational programs have a life span of 1-2 years unless handled in an exceptional manner.)

Deborah worked at a newspaper in Northern California. She constantly made great suggestions to improve circulation of the paper and increase print advertising. Deborah had been a solid performer since she had started to work for the paper as a cub reporter in the early 1970's. She had received every reward that the company provided on a regular basis. After a particularly important suggestion, the editor of the paper decided to give Deborah a "special recognition" that she knew Deborah would appreciate.

She invited Deborah's husband and 2 children to work on a Friday afternoon and at a hastily called "all hands meeting," she handed Deborah a unique front page of the newspaper. On that edition of the day's paper, not available to the public, was a picture of Deborah, along with her suggestion in bold print as the headline of the page. A front page story accompanied the picture. This was later framed and handed to Deborah in front of her family and peers. The tears streaming down Deborah's face indicated just how much she appreciated being recognized by the editor and the paper. You can be assured that, when Deborah is asked to stay late to complete a task, she will do so with a broad smile on her face.

3)   AVERAGE

In one sense, these people are the hardest people to motivate. They are getting their jobs done. There isn't exceptional performance, yet they are accomplishing what is expected from them. No more. No less. They are steady and consistent in what they do. They don't often volunteer for new tasks or seem to enjoy them. They thrive on repeatable, routine tasks. They just want to put in their time and then go home. Don't stand in front of the exit to their offices at 5:00 PM unless you enjoy the prospect of being trampled to death by the herd of Average employees clocking out at 5:00 on the dot. They are very sensitive to changes where they believe that they are being asked to do "more" than their counterparts. They will remind you that "everyone is being paid the same amount, so everyone should do exactly the same amount of work." Every Average employee seems to keep a close watch on what every other Average employee is doing. You will hear about it if they sense that someone else is "getting away with doing less" than they are.

What motivates Average employees?

While Water Walkers feel suffocated by order, rules and structure, Average employees thrive on these guidelines. They delight in knowing what is expected and doing it. They often hoard knowledge from others and are reluctant to share what they know with others for fear that if they are successful at training another employee to do their job, they may be asked to do something else.

Routines, though limiting to other employees, are preferred here. If Sally is used to coming into work, checking her email and then wandering over to the coffee machine for her caffeine fix, heaven help the new leader who wants to start the day with a morning huddle. He can expect to see Sally, either arriving late on a regular basis or tapping her pencil repeatedly (or some other repeated random energy gesture) throughout the entire meeting, while she daydreams about that delightful first sip of her black coffee with one sugar but no cream.

Don't get me wrong. We need Average employees. After all, there is much routine work that needs to be completed in the workplace. And there is a lot to be said for consistency and replicability at work. However, when change must be made, the Average employee will sit there with a big "Wait and See" attitude before climbing aboard. They are not likely to be early adopters or even secondary adopters of the change. Some of them will have to be dragged kicking and screaming into the change. More likely, they will "Wait and See" how others adapt to the change. When resistance seems futile, they will reluctantly get on the train. Don't put them in charge of your "Employee Suggestion Program" unless you really don't want to get or implement a lot of changes.

I often speak at award banquets where long-term employees receive service pins for valued years of consistent service. When I shake the hands of 25- or 30-year employees, I am pleasantly surprised to hear them tell me how much they enjoyed coming to work each and every day, knowing exactly what they had to do and doing it.

Wilson loaded UPS Truck #174 almost every work day for 26 years for Sammy, who drove that same truck and delivered those packages almost every work day for the same 26 years. Yes, they both took vacations, but they almost never used sick time or took unnecessary time off. When they spoke about their jobs, they both beamed with pride, imagining the customers on the upper West Side in NYC who valued and appreciated receiving their packages in a timely fashion. Even the ones marked "fragile."

UnCommon Sense tells us that whatever floats your boat and gets the job done (as long as it doesn't hurt others) is fine and should be appreciated. Wilson and Sammy were both model employees. They did their jobs. No more. No less. UPS was fortunate to have more solid citizens like Wilson and Sammy, as opposed to a character like me. At least the people on the West Side got their packages in one piece.

4) AVERAGE MINUS EMPLOYEES

Although these employees are not currently performing up to speed, leaders need to focus most of their available leadership time on this group of employees. You will get the greatest ROIT working with the Average Minus employee. 80% of Average Minus employees can be raised up to the Average level with the proper treatment. 15% have the potential to become Average Plus employees. That can turn around the morale of the entire work team quickly. There is no other type of employee group where that level of ROIT can be attained.

Who are Average Minus employees?

We all recognize that there are employees in the workplace who just don't quite seem to cut it. They can do most of their work, but they can't ever do all of their work. They are forever falling short on either a task or in a work relationship. Something always gets in their way. There are usually a lot of excuses about why the work isn't finished. The excuses are tired, and these employees rarely take ownership for their lack of performance. The worst part of this is that they often believe they are Average Plus performers.

What does the Common Sense leader do with the Average Minus employees? Usually the work gets reassigned to the Average Plus employees, who begrudgingly complete it. What do the Average Minus employees get? They rarely have to face the fact that they are not helping the team and getting the job done. Often, here are no real consequences at all which guarantees that this behavior will continue unabated.

What motivates Average Minus employees?

Here is where it gets interesting and where you need UnCommon Sense. There are 2 sets of factors that account for Average Minus performance. One set of factors has to do with the manner in which the Average Minus employee is being led. The other set of factors has to do with the employee himself/herself.

Which leadership factors account for subpar performance?

a) Unclear or unexplained expectations;
b) Inadequate training;
c) Constantly shifting expectations;
d) Not being held accountable for performance; and
e) Lack of coaching and support.

Which employee factors account for subpar performance?

a) FOF (fear of failure);
b) Extreme sensitivity to critique (either due to parents, past teachers, past bosses, friends or current bosses);
c) Low self-esteem;
d) Knowledge barriers; and
e) Oil/vinegar personality/work style mismatches with co-workers or leaders.

However, if there was one driving factor that takes center stage in all of this, it would have to be FOF/Fear Of Failure. Nothing gets in the way of success more than perceived thoughts and concerns about non-success/failure.

Consider the following 2 situations:

When I was 24, I was named Principal of an elementary school. Before you ask "Wait a minute. How did you get a job as a principal at 24? Didn't you have to be older and have more experience?" Let me clarify and say that I became the secular principal at a local, religious private, elementary/junior high school. To become a principal in the public school system, I would most definitely have had to pay my dues as a teacher, lower level administrator and vice principal and learn to hate children along the way.

In the private school system, the requirements are a bit different. I was hired because I was completing my doctorate. They were looking for someone who had experience in elementary school. I also shared the religious affiliation with the school. Most importantly, I knew someone high up on the board of directors. It didn't hurt that I had spent more than 3 years working as a substitute teacher in inner city schools as well. Additionally, I was willing to work for substandard wages and had the 2 requisite skills that were needed to be successful. I was told by the chairperson of the board that I would be considered successful if I:

a) Kept the children happy and
b) Kept the Board from getting too many complaints from parents who equated paying for their child's education with knowing something about exceptional educational practices.

I didn't know any better, so I took the job.

We had a 3rd grade boy, Micah, who was clearly not the sharpest pencil in the box. He wasn't stupid, but he wasn't Albert Einstein either. The subject he really didn't like was Social Studies. Now 3rd grade Social Studies is not rocket science. For those who have forgotten or never completed 3rd grade, here is a quick review. Columbus. Nina. Pinta. Santa Maria. Pilgrims. Pocahontas. Washington. Revolutionary War. Lincoln. Civil War. End of 3rd grade Social Studies.

What Micah especially didn't like was taking tests in Social Studies. Here is what he would do. Whenever, he took a test in Social Studies, Micah had a routine. He would look at the first question on the test. If he couldn't answer that question, he would look at the last question. If he couldn't answer that question either, he would tear his paper up. This was actually quite logical.

Since he knew that his parents, Mr. and Mrs. Cro-Magnon, would beat him if he failed a test, he simply opted not to take the test if he thought that he might fail. You might have reached a similar conclusion if you had met his parents.

All he suffered from was FOF, manifesting itself as test anxiety. We called his parents in to talk with them about what to do. Their response was predictable. They said, "No problem. Just hit him in school when he does that and that will stop him. That's what we do with him at home." We said, "We don't believe in that and we don't hit children at our school. It is not consistent with how we think kids learn." They said, "Well you should hit the kids when they misbehave." I responded that we were not a Catholic school. OK, that was a joke, but you get the point here.

So how did we get Micah to take his Social Studies tests?

Whenever I ask this question in front of an audience, I usually get the same suggestions, such as:

1) Don't tell him it is a test.
   (You know there are tests in the world. I definitely want there to be tests of competence in the world. When I go in to have brain surgery, I want a doctor who has passed all of his tests demonstrating exceptional skill and capability before I let him drill open my head and mess with my brain. Micah will have to take tests for the rest of his academic career and maybe beyond, so we will have to tell him that this IS A TEST.)
2) Let him take the test orally.
   (I love that one. Now we can add public humiliation to what is already a desperate situation.)
3) Cheerlead for him to build up his confidence.
   (OK, imagine the teacher telling him that he is going to do well. Positive words work well with children who have a successful track record. They are not nearly as effective with children like Micah who have not been as successful. Words won't easily erase the picture of Mom and/or Dad hitting him with a strap.)

None of these suggestions would do much good.

Consider that the only antidote for FAILURE is SUCCESS. How can we increase his chances of success?

How about by starting with an easy first question such as "What nationality was Nick the Greek?" After he gets that one right, he will go to the last question. How about using "What color was George Washington's white horse?" Bingo. Two for Two.

If we throw in a slightly harder question at Question #2 on the test, his thoughts about failure may have disappeared or at least been reduced. Why? Because he has evidence that he is now succeeding.

Psychologists know that once a person has had a string of 3 running successes, his/her thoughts about failure are diminished. By structuring success into his journey, we can help Micah overcome his concerns about failure. The classical name for this is SSPS (Successful Sequential Problem Solving.) Need a simpler name? How about 3 Successes in a Row?

The second example is not from the world of work, but it provides another example of 3 successes in a row. Like any good parent, I wanted my daughter, Rebecca, to learn to swim at a young age. I had her in the pool before she was 1-year-old, and she was happy and unafraid as she swam.

By the time, she was, I told her that I would now teach her to swim underwater. She would have to put her entire head under the water, hold her breath and then swim. A look of horror flashed on her face as she quickly said, "No way."

There is a lesson in this. Whenever you ask someone or even YOURSELF to do something and the automatic knee jerk answer is "no/no way/no how" or anything like that, seemingly without thought, it tells you that this person is afraid of something, that fear has raised its ugly head again.

When I asked Rebecca what was making her afraid, she responded with "Nothing." Another sure sign that fear was present. So what would a 4-year-old be afraid of?

Don't say drowning. That is an adult idea. Few 4-year-olds know what drowning is. Maybe she was afraid that there were monsters or sharks in the water. We were swimming in a pool, so that wasn't likely. How about that she would sink to the bottom of the pool? Maybe she was concerned about not being able to see and would bump her head against the side of the pool. All of these are at least within the realm of possibilities.

Have you ever watched Saturday morning cartoons with your children? Have you ever seen what happens to a cartoon character (other than Sponge Bob and his friends) when they go into the water? Water fills up inside of their head and when they come out, the water flies out through a variety of orifices in their head. To an adult, this is just silly. To a small child, this may be scary. They don't know how to get the water out of their head. No one has ever taught them how to do that.

After much questioning, Rebecca finally blurted out in an exasperated way, "Look, I have seven holes in my head. Water is going to fill up my head and that will be the end of me." In case you haven't counted the holes in your head recently, you have 2 eyes, 2 ears, 2 nostrils and a mouth. The good news was that at least she could count to seven. The bad news was that there was no way/no how that she was going to put her head under the water.

Most dads would have responded in the "typical Dad" way. They would have hurled poor Rebecca into the pool. After all, that is probably the way they learned to swim. And Rebecca may have quickly learned that she could swim under water and that her head did not fill up with water. Then again, she might have hated Dad (an unacceptable option for me) and never gone into the pool again. I wasn't willing to take that chance.

Common Sense dictates that I should have taken out a medical textbook and explained the protective features in her head such as ear drums, nasal membranes and eyelids, all designed to keep water out of her head. Typical of logic people. Trying to solve an EMOTIONAL issue with LOGIC. Remember using logic, when someone is afraid or upset only serves to annoy or infuriate that person.

What would YOU have done if you wanted her to have a successful experience the very first time she put her head under the water? Remember, we are looking for inch stones or centimeter stones, not mile stones.

UnCommon Sense gave me the idea of going to the local pharmacy and buying EACH OF US a pair of goggles, nose clips and a set of ear plugs. I put them on myself and took Rebecca over to the full-length mirror in her room. I showed her how to put her set on and asked her to look at herself in the mirror. I asked her to check the holes in her head and see if they were all covered. She said, "Well it looks like 6 holes are covered, but what about my mouth?" I said, "Keep that shut, and we'll be fine." We both looked a bit like goons, but the holes in her head were less of an issue. I asked her if she was ready to swim underwater and she tentatively said she would give it a go.

She looked a bit goofy but swam like a fish the first time out. Why? Because she was no longer thinking about FAILURE. She could see clearly with the goggles and loved the idea of fishing things out from the bottom of the pool. Shortly after, she pulled out the ear plugs because she didn't like them. The nose clip followed. She kept the goggles on so that she could see better.

The kicker to the story is that when I ask her today, "Rebecca, do you remember when you were afraid to put your head under the water?" Her response is, "Dad, I was never afraid." She NEVER HAD TO EXPERIENCE THE FEAR because it was taken out of the situation before she could experience it.

5) HUMAN SPEED BUMPS

Sadly, these folks are the bottom feeders of your organization. On a ROIT basis, less than 20% of them are recoverable back to the Average level. They do the least amount of work and are the least committed to organizational goals. They are actually quite proud of that fact as well. If they are allowed to impact others, they can truly become a cancerous, malignant tumor to your organization. You know that a person is a Human Speed Bump if it takes them an hour and a half to watch the CBS television show "60 Minutes."

Human Speed Bumps often drive to work in a pickup truck that has a bumper sticker prominently displayed on their truck which says: "The worst day fishing is better than the best day working." I have nothing against fishing, but sitting in a boat being too drunk to fish during a rainstorm is not better than my job. The message here is that Human Speed Bumps often get their enjoyment in life from their off-hours activities as opposed to their at-work activities.

What motivates Human Speed Bumps?

This is fairly simple. Doing as little as possible AND getting away with it. Human Speed Bumps will spend more time trying to get out of work or avoiding a task that they don't like than it would take to actually complete the work. Their pride comes from work avoidance more so than from work completion. The sad part is that leaders spend far too much time dealing with these employees. AND they don't deal with them effectively. Yes, there needs to documentation of non-performance, but that isn't likely to improve performance. It will just make it easier and more legally acceptable to discipline or fire them.

Here is the UnCommon Sense. The reason to deal with Human Speed Bumps is not for their benefit. It is for the benefit of the other employees, mostly for the Average Plus, who strongly resent that these people are getting away with murder, while the Average Plus employees are working to exhaustion to compensate for the Human Speed Bumps' lack of performance. A leader who actively deals with

Human Speed Bumps will instantly move up on the Average Plus Hero Scale.

So what should you do?

Holding these employees accountable will make them quite uncomfortable. I usually encourage leaders to move their desks next to Human Speed Bumps and shorten their leash considerably. If you restrict their freedom to "NOT WORK," this will have a great impact on them. This is not easy to do. In reality, you have to convince them that you need them to work and care about them working much more than they care about not working. You will need to hold them accountable for 40 hours of work for 40 hours of pay.

Remember that they care A LOT about NOT WORKING. This task is not for the faint-hearted or weak-willed leader. DO NOT EVEN THINK ABOUT STARTING TO DO THIS UNLESS YOU ARE WILLING TO MAKE A COMMITMENT TO YOURSELF AND TO THEM TO SEE IT THROUGH TO ITS LOGICAL END. There may be grievances. There may be lots of overtime where you actually complete your own job (since you will be spending your regular work hours getting on their cases.)

It involves writing measurable behavioral contracts, constant monitoring, training and constant status checking. Usually these employees, after a few grievances, will ask for a transfer to a less disciplined leader. Most leaders are not willing to invest all of this time. Instead they spend their time compensating for the Human Speed Bumps' lack of productivity. The choice is yours.

The more Human Speed Bumps are allowed to get away with, the more the impact begins to spread to the Average Minus employee and even to the Average employee. At some point, even Average Plus employees just give up and stop doing all of the extra work that they have been asked to complete. Not a pretty picture.

UnCommon Sense says it is better to deal directly with the Human Speed Bumps and move them along than to allow them to poison the rest of the group. How many Human Speed Bumps do you have to deal with BEFORE everyone gets the picture? One? Don't be that naive. The first Human Speed Bump you deal with will get other people to think that you just didn't like that person. By the time you deal with the second Human Speed Bump, they will start to sense a theme developing here. By the time you deal with the third Human Speed Bump, they'll start to get the idea that "you are working your way back to them."

THOUGHT BOMBS TO PONDER

1) Think of your own organization and how people fit into the five categories that I have described. Are you recognizing the payoffs for each group of employees? Are you providing an environment that is conducive to getting the maximum amount of performance out of each group? Where are you spending your leadership time? Are you getting a 300% to 500% ROIT on your leadership time? Are you using Common or UnCommon Sense?

2) For Your Water Walkers: Look around your office. Is it set up to foster creativity? Is it set up to help your Water Walkers seek out and attack challenging problems and issues? Is there enough challenging work to keep them actively engaged?

3) For Your Average Plus Employees: Does your organization provide recognitions to these employees who are truly unique? Does your organization touch its employees' hearts on a regular basis? While Average Plus employees claim that they don't need "a parade and a statue" just for doing their job, they do crave thoughtful, sincere and honest recognition.

(Note: However, you won't get your largest ROIT from these employees because they are already doing yeoman's work. There isn't that much more that you can ask from them without burning them out.)

4) For Your Average Employees: Does your organization have a place for people like Wilson and Sammy? Look at the jobs that require consistency and reliability. Are they staffed with people who thrive on structure and predictability? Selecting

the right person for the right job goes a long way. The only caution I can offer is that a manager will not get the greatest ROIT from time invested in these employees either.

5) For Your Average Minus Employees: Are you the type of leader who can grow these employees into Average or even Average Plus employees? Are you willing to spend your time sequencing work properly (3 successes in a row) to maximize their chances for success? Are you willing to spend your time coaching and cheerleading for these Average Minus employees when they are frightened of failure? This kind of leadership behavior consists of taking new tasks or tasks not being completed in a successful manner and breaking them down into tiny pieces where the Average Minus employee can have early successes and not be consumed by thoughts of failure. Combining SSPS with skillful, coaching, feedback and a bit of PMA (Positive Mental Attitude) can restore energy, vitality and most importantly, performance enhancement for the Average Minus employee.

6) For The Human Speed Bump Employees: Are you willing to confront their bad behavior knowing that they may file a grievance? Are you willing to watch over them carefully and possibly incur lots of extra work to make sure they stop getting away with not working? Are you willing to ride this out for the long run? Do you care more about them working than they care about NOT working?

CHAPTER 5

PROVIDING THE RIGHT AMOUNT OF FREEDOM

COMMON SENSE

If you want an employee to get things done correctly, you must plan, organize, direct and control what they do. Set the proper expectations so that employees can meet them.

UNCOMMON SENSE

There is a lot to be said for setting high expectations for performance. However, once those expectations are set, get the heck out of the way and let the employee figure out how to actually meet them.

While some employees prefer to have their lives organized for them by their leaders, more employees enjoy the challenge that comes from solving complex problems themselves. This is particularly true for Gen X and Gen Y, who thrive on solving problems. UnCommon Sense suggests that the closer the person is to the problem, the easier it is for them to grasp the real underlying issues and solve the problem. If problems are escalated to people with offices, far from the line of fire, the solutions may not be as practical, and there will be far less buy in of these solutions from "boots on the ground" personnel.

When I was the Director of Leadership Development at a high technology company, I was ultimately transferred to work for a Senior Vice President of Finance named Waldo. He had little awareness of what I did on a day-to-day basis. Waldo was too busy dealing with financial issues to take an interest in the subject matter I was presenting to attendees at my training programs. The only contact that I had with him was the ritual of having him sign my timecard each week. This struck me as odd because I routinely charged 40 hours per week to the exact same "overhead" account each week.

There was no delineation as to what I was doing whatsoever. Waldo demanded that I show up each Friday in his office around 3:00 PM for the signing ritual. This was never accompanied by questions or suggestions.

As a director-level employee, it seemed quite demeaning to me. I constantly questioned why I had to show up at his office for my weekly 5-minute "nonversation." Waldo responded that this was his way of making sure that I was doing what I was supposed to be doing. Huh?? I usually responded back by saying, "When you clip a free bird's wings, they usually grow back bigger each time." I suspect that the metaphor was lost on Waldo, but after 3 months of this back and forth wrestling for control of my time card, I was shifted to another leader who took a much greater interest in what I was up to.

Consider these folks:

Enos worked as a route driver delivering sandwiches to convenience stores in two southern states. He was just one of 145 drivers who were never allowed to "sell" the product to store owners. That task was left to a professional sales force of 5 individuals. Each of them had a huge territory and barely got a chance to visit each store owner more than once a quarter. The members of the sales force would check in with each owner weekly on the telephone, but face-to-face contact for the sales force was limited to approximately four times a year.

Why were the drivers not allowed to "sell" sandwiches? Common Sense dictated that they were just drivers, not trained sales personnel. Not to belittle the "professional" sales force, but selling 15 different types of sandwiches is not brain surgery. Margins were small, so the key issue for company success was volume. For reasons that no one understood, tastes in sandwiches were regionalized and seemed to shift for unexplained reasons. Egg salad sold in one area, while bologna was king in other areas. Po' boys seemed to sell all over the South.

I asked the leadership team why they were limiting their sales force to 5 people when there were 30 times more people who could get involved in the sales effort with just a bit of training. What would you rather have? A sales team of 5 or a sales team of 150? After a bit of convincing, they agreed to let the route drivers try their hand at "selling" sandwiches.

Enos enjoyed eating "po' boys" as much as any sandwich. He took it upon himself to start sharing his sandwiches with some of the store owners. As you know, "breaking bread" is a great way to build rapport. Enos showed how much he enjoyed eating his sandwich, and this seemed to impress enough store owners to increase the number of "po' boys" that they carried in their stores by 11%. Not bad for a driver with only a few hours of sales training. The real kicker was that Enos enjoyed his job more, gained 10 pounds from eating more "po' boys" and was looking forward to receiving more training. His self-esteem also shot up because he no longer saw himself as "just a driver."

Annie worked as a night teller at a local bank. Now banks are not the most progressive organizations on the face of the earth. In fact, some bankers are not very smart at all. Some of them leave their vaults wide open BUT chain the pens down in the lobby. Seems to me like they are protecting the wrong resources.

Annie worked in the world of credit. Whenever a customer requested an increase in their credit line, she transferred the request to a junior vice president, who would review the account and make the credit decision. Now in most banks, there are just two job titles: tellers and 6 levels of vice presidents. Being a vice president at some banks just means that you are no longer a teller. Nothing to write home about.

Annie always wondered why she couldn't make the same decision as the Jr. VP. She finally asked her boss if he would allow her to take a shot at making credit decisions on small increase requests. With all credit records automated and available at every bankers' fingertips, her boss gave her general guidelines and a few specific questions to ask borrowers.

Much to everyone's surprise (or maybe to no one's surprise), Annie was able to reach the identical credit decision as the VP (on requests involving $5K or less increases) more than 90% of the time within 2 months. Yes, there were some exceptional customers with exceptional circumstances that dictated more thoughtful credit decisions. However, by empowering Annie, the Jr. VP was able spend his time on those issues and spend more time on more strategic issues.

Annie felt much better about her job because she felt she was no longer "just a teller." Annie liked the fact that she was held accountable for her decisions. She enjoyed explaining her conclusions and reasons for her decisions to her boss and anyone else who asked. She found her job more stimulating and began thinking about going back to college to get a degree in finance.

Have you created an environment where employees are encouraged to make their own decisions? Red Lion Hotels armed 40% of their on-site employees with a "Yes, I Can" button. Wearers of that button were empowered to do anything and everything to satisfy customer requests up to "comping" their room for the night. Customers were delighted that the MOD (Manager on Duty) did not have to approve these requests. Anyone with a button could do so. Once again, employees were held accountable for their decisions. They also were proud of their ability to respond quickly and directly to customer concerns.

Would you agree that employees like to feel that they have some control over what happens in their environment? Want to try an interesting experiment?

Spend a day asking random employees one question over and over again. The question is "Why are you doing that?" In the beginning, employees will have a quick, rather pat answer. If you persist, at some point, they will throw their hands up into the air and scream, "I have no idea why I am doing that."

Make sure that everyone knows what they are doing and why they are doing it. It makes for stronger levels of buy in, commitment and productivity.

THOUGHT BOMBS TO PONDER

1) Who makes the decisions in your organization? How about the small decisions?

2) What is keeping you from empowering employees and holding them accountable for decisions? Do you trust them enough to grow them into making more complex decisions? (Note: It is interesting to note that many empowerment campaigns have failed. Even though empowerment is a great concept, it is typically "poorly" sold to employees. Employees who do not understand the vision of the organization and are not bought in to what is going on may need to be educated and energized before any empowerment campaign will have a chance to work. To most employees, empowerment means more work without any more pay.)

3) What kind of training will be necessary for your employees to be able to step up and make decisions? Have you thought about decision trees and other tools that can teach your employees about how to "think and decide" on a different level?

4) Have you considered the merits and demerits of micromanaging your employees and leaving them little or no career path? When there is no career path for your employees, how loyal will they be to the organizations?

5) Are you worried that teaching your employees how to do parts of your job will render you less important? Have you thought about offering to learn how to do part of your boss's job?

Enough about motivation.

Let's talk about the way in which we can optimize communication.

CHAPTER 6

EMOTIONS SPEAK LOUDER THAN FACTS

COMMON SENSE

As LAPD Sgt. Joe Friday (Dragnet) used to say: "All we want are the facts. Just the facts, ma'am."

UNCOMMON SENSE

Facts do matter, but feelings matter more. If you don't deal with the feelings FIRST, the facts are less likely to be believed and accepted.

When we communicate with others, we organize our thoughts around the data/facts we are going to communicate. This assumes that the world we live in is factual and logical. While there are many logical elements to communication, dealing with the emotional side of things FIRST can set the climate for a more fruitful conversation.

Think of how the person listening to you is feeling about you, your organization or the message you are about to deliver. Wouldn't you "frame the message" differently if you felt that they liked you as opposed to disliked you? Think about it this way. When you try to apply logic to emotional issues without first understanding feelings, it tends to infuriate the person who is in the midst of experiencing their emotions. They will not be likely to hear or agree with your facts.

Consider this common example. In many relationships, one person is more emotional, while the other person is more logical. There is nothing inherently wrong or problematic with this, until the emotional person has a problem. In male-female relationships, women (for a variety of reasons including that they are more open, aware and enlightened) tend to be more emotional than their male counterparts. When I try to explain this to women, I tell them it may be helpful to view the men in their lives as well-intentioned, emotionally primitive individuals (basically pigs with shoes). I am not saying this to judge men badly. After all, I am a guy. It is just a way of describing how differently men and women (or logical and emotional people) view the same situation.

If the woman comes home upset about something that has happened during the day and relates this to her male partner, he will respond by doing what he "thinks" will make her feel better. Therefore, he will first logically explain to her why she shouldn't be upset in the first place. Often, he unwittingly implies that she has caused her own upset by not being logical. This is a logical, Common Sense driven way to see the problem, but doesn't provide the active listening and empathy that she is seeking

Most women will listen to this and think, "What did I ever see in this guy? How did I ever allow myself to get involved with this fool in the first place?" Seeing that his first reaction has not solved the situation, the man will then offer to "help to fix the problem" despite the fact that this is NOT what the woman asked for. He is subtly implying that, since she can't solve the problem by herself, he will do it for her. Of course, in return, he expects to be rewarded and appreciated, while the woman looks for a heavy metal object to hurl at his head to show her disdain for what has just happened. The real answer to this issue is to have a chat about the different ways in which you both look at things in a Venus-Mars conversation. Easier said than done. If this conversation can be held at a neutral time, each side might be able to better understand the dynamics of the situation.

This is not just true in male/female interactions. Examples abound in the business world as well. Consider these examples:

Victoria was a Senior Level Executive working in the public sector, helping to guide an agency that delivered health care to low-income families with sick children. There were 75 employees in this organization, and the vast majority of them were women. The office was multicultural with employees from over 10 different countries. Employees included nurses, clerical staff and financial analysts.

Victoria walked through the hallways of the office every morning and cordially greeted everyone who was there. By doing this, she thought that she was providing plenty of the "warm fuzzies" to her staff. At one all-hands meeting, an issue came up. There was an anonymous note from an employee explaining that she felt offended that she was not "re-greeted" by Victoria later in the afternoon. The employee was concerned that Victoria had walked right by her without so much as an acknowledgement. Victoria was flabbergasted.

Privately, she said, "How many times a day do I need to say hello to everyone here? Are they just that insecure?" She asked for suggestions as to how to "fix the problem." Options suggested by her leadership staff included:

1) Take an afternoon walk through the office and "re-greet" everyone again.
2) Stay in her office for most of the afternoon.
3) Tell the staff to stop whining, put on their big girl panties and get back to work.

All of these suggestions dealt with the "facts" about "re-greeting" employees. I pointed out that no one was considering how the employees were feeling. UnCommon Sense tells us that when we argue about small, seemingly trivial things, those are usually not the "real/bottom line issues." The small slights may just be easier to talk about, but they are just the tip of the iceberg. Lots of the time, the real "elephant in the room" is apparent to everyone, but no one is quite willing to address it directly.

I went out and sought opinions from many of the employees about how they felt about working at the agency and how they felt about Victoria as well. I can't say that I was surprised to hear that, although employees liked the agency and were proud of the health care that was being delivered, that they felt that Victoria was "cold and aloof" at times. They felt that, although she regularly asked for their suggestions, those suggestions were rarely implemented. Asking for suggestions seemed to represent more "lip service" than real interest in how the employees felt. For cultural and political reasons, employees did not feel comfortable approaching Victoria with these concerns. So Victoria ended up viewing the problem as a "re-greeting" problem, as opposed to a "perception of her openness" problem.

Once Victoria became aware of the real issue and calmed down about how she felt, she was able to address the "real" issue at the next all-hands meeting. A suggestion evaluation committee, made up of front line employees, was implemented to review all suggestions. Many of the suggestions were implemented in short order. "Re-greeting" became less and less of an issue. Victoria started to spend more of her time listening to employees as opposed to just greeting them. When Victoria was able to understand and deal with the "hurt" feelings of her employees, the "factual" issue of re-greeting all but disappeared.

Here is another example:

In the mid 1980's, Roland was a 50+-year-old engineer working for a high technology company on the West Coast. He had been married for over 20 years, had raised 2 sons with his wife and had been a model employee for his 12 years with the company.

Much to everyone's surprise, Roland walked into the office of the VP of engineering one Monday and announced that he wanted to live true to his heart and soul and become the woman whom he knew he really was -- Rolanda. Unknown to everyone were the following facts:

a) Roland(a) had been divorced from his wife for more than 3 years;
b) Roland(a) had waited to seek surgery until after his last son was away at college;
c) Roland(a) had never used a urinal in his life. Every time he had gone to the restroom, he had always sat down;
d) Roland(a) had been cross dressing as a woman everywhere but at work for the past 3 years; and
e) Roland(a) had already consulted with his/her doctor, who thought she/he should cross dress everywhere for a year

prior to having surgery, just to make sure that he/she was absolutely certain about her/his choice.

Although this was a liberal, progressive company, you can imagine the stir that was created in the wake of this announcement. The first flashpoint of contention whenever this situation arises is a rather mundane issue, namely, which bathroom Roland(a) would use during the year that he/she cross-dressed prior to surgery.

Because this is such a challenging issue for most companies, well over 90% of transgender individuals will leave their current place of employment and seek work elsewhere. Roland(a) was such a strong employee that it would have been a shame to see her/him leave.

The VP of HR asked for my input after unsuccessfully trying the following 4 options:

1) Converting all of the bathrooms in the facility into unisex bathrooms (this lasted for less than 2 hours);
2) Encouraging Roland(a) to use only the male restrooms;
3) Encouraging Roland(a) to use only the female restrooms;
4) Encouraging Roland(a) to use the bathroom closest to his/her office.

The key point here is that the issue is not really about bathroom usage at all. If we focus only on the "facts" of bathroom usage, we miss the more important issue of how everyone was feeling. And there were a lot of feelings about this topic. They ranged from:

a) As long as Roland(a) doesn't bother me, I don't care which bathroom, she/he uses;
b) I don't want Roland(a) to come on to me in the men's/women's bathroom;
c) This is the devil's work. It is a perversion. I don't want to have anything to do with Roland(a).

Quite a range of viewpoints, wouldn't you agree?

UnCommon Sense dictates that if we can deal with how people feel FIRST, then we can find a more suitable way to deal with the "facts" of the situation. To accomplish this, several things happened:

1) Informational meetings about "transgender" individuals were held with men and women separately. Everyone who chose to attend the meetings was encouraged to ask questions, although no one was permitted to ask questions specifically about Roland(a) in order to protect his/her right to privacy. Interesting information was provided to all attendees such as the fact that due to the hormonal treatments that Roland(a) was receiving prior to surgery, she/he was largely asexual and not likely to approach either men or women in a sexual manner.

2) The company wanted everyone to know that their rights to THINK whatever they wanted about Roland(a) would be protected. Courtesy would be shown to Roland(a)'s supporters and non-supporters equally as long as those opinions were not broadcast and shared publically (an early form of Don't Ask, Don't Tell.)

3) It was made clear that the most important issue was that the work continue as seamlessly as possible. Employees working directly with Roland(a) who felt uncomfortable being with her/him were offered a "buffer" person to serve as a liaison between Roland(a) and that person.

Here is the beauty of the story. Despite strong verbal protests in the beginning, once it was known that the company would attempt to HONOR EVERYONE'S FEELINGS, the issue of the bathroom no longer dominated everyone's attention. Here were a few of outcomes:

1) Roland(a) agreed to use only single stall restrooms for the first 11 months of the year in return for the company campaigning to their health insurance provider to cover the costs of surgery under the diagnosis of "Gender Dysphoria." The insurance company agreed to do so.

2) Because Roland(a) was a positive, well-liked employee, most of his/her colleagues quickly accepted the new situation. Roland(a) confided to her/his closest colleagues that she had begun to feel like Dolly Parton compared to the way she looked before, as she began to receive hormonal treatments.

3) NO ONE ASKED FOR A BUFFER PERSON TO WORK WITH ROLAND(A).

4) Most importantly, Roland(a) was able to continue working for the organization for at least 3 years, after which I no longer had contact with Rolanda and the organization.

If we constantly remember to deal with emotions BEFORE dealing with facts, our communications are more likely to deal effectively with the facts. While some people pride themselves on being like Sgt. Joe Friday and dealing directly with the facts, almost every piece of communication has emotional overtones or undertones. Those of you who are sensitive to this will become better leaders and communicators.

Leaders often are uncomfortable dealing with their own emotions as well as the emotions of others. Common Sense tells us the emotions are a sign that people are not thinking clearly and making decisions objectively. UnCommon Sense tells us that there is now physiological and psychological evidence that emotions underlie most of our conscious thought processes. We all make decisions emotionally and usually justify those decisions with logic.

As a leader, do you understand and concern yourself with the emotional issues of your workplace? Do you understand how your employees feel? Do you know what "elephant in the room" issues may be masquerading as "facts?" When it comes time for you to communicate your hopes and vision for your group, can you do so in a way that resonates with the hearts and minds of your employees? Those leaders who can make the appeal in an emotional manner as well as in a factual/logical manner will be more likely to be successful.

THOUGHT BOMBS TO PONDER

1) When you think back to the last 3 unpleasant conversations that you have had at work or at home, which aspect of the issue did you focus on first? The factual aspect? Or the emotional aspect? Have you noticed that when you deal with how people feel before you try to process the factual information that you are more likely to solve the issue quickly?

2) What is uncomfortable about dealing with emotions? Are you concerned that the other person will yell at you? Become angry? Quickly lose control of the situation?

3) When you are discussing unhappy customers, staff or Senior Management, what type of remedies are considered first? Emotional remedies? Or Factual remedies?

4) When people around you react (or overreact) strongly to comparatively small issues, do you respond directly to those issues, or do you attempt to understand their feelings and delve below the surface?

5) When you plan your communications, do you consider the emotional tempo of the situation that you are walking into or do you use the same presentation regardless of the mood of the audience?

CHAPTER 7

THE LESS SAID, THE BETTER

COMMON SENSE

The more complete you are in the way in which you communicate, the more likely that everyone will understand what you are saying. You can show others how smart and clever you are by explaining everything in great detail.

UNCOMMON SENSE

The best messages are short and sweet. They are direct and to the point. The best messages use EMOTIONALLY EVOCATIVE LANGUAGE, directed at the heart AND the head.

How many times have you heard someone continue to speak ad nauseum about a topic that only they were interested in? They keep giving you more and more information, well past the point of your interest. You kept wanting to say TMI (Too Much Information), but politeness prevented you from doing so. You resort to looking at your watch, doodling "KMN" (Kill Me NOW) on your notepad or needlessly checking your "crackberry" (read *BlackBerry*) to no avail. You would like to refer the person to the self-help group "On and On and On." The other person is oblivious to your plight and keeps on keeping on.

Consider these examples:

Mike has sold fishing boats at a mid-Atlantic dealership for over 15 years. He thinks he is a great salesperson, a true legend in his own mind. Now don't get me wrong. He has sold a lot of boats. but I know that he could have sold even more boats, if he had ever stopped to analyze his communication style.

Mike knows a lot about fishing. He loves to go fishing himself and drives to work every day in a Ford pickup truck with the "I'd rather be fishing" bumper sticker affixed to his right rear bumper. He knows everything about the brands of boats that he sells as well as everything about the brands of what his competitors sell. He can steer boats, fix them and could probably take one apart and put it back together again in short order. If a customer wants to talk for hours about boats, Mike is the sales guy for him.

The only problem is that apparently, Mike was born without ears or dislikes listening to some of his customers. He just likes to "talk to them." Or more so, "talk at them." I watched Mike chat with a potential customer and later asked him if he thought he was being paid by the word. That would have certainly explained why Mike was going into agonizing and painstaking detail about the dimensions of the boat, the specs of the engines and the intricacies of the electronics on the boat.

All of that might have been terrific if the potential buyer also really knew a lot about boats and cared about these details. When Mike asked for feedback on his selling style, I told him, "Mike, you have so much knowledge about boats. There are really pearls of wisdom in so much of what you have to say. However, the pearls are buried amidst tons of crap (read *extra words*) that may cause the customer to miss some of the really important stuff." Great sales people speak 1/3 of the time, allowing their customers to speak 2/3 of the time. Great sales people ask great questions, listen intently and then make short concise, emotionally powerful responses. Mike, apparently, never got that memo.

The particular customer whom I watched Mike deal with was a first time customer more interested in the "boating experience" than he was in the boat. Mike thought that the more he spoke about the boat, the more informed he would appear to the customer. Mike failed to listen and really hear the customer when he described "the perfect day for him." He missed the gleam in the customer's eyes when he said that a "perfect day" would be for him and his buddies to be sitting on a boat in the middle of the river at 6:00 AM, the sun just starting to shine, beers and ham sandwiches in everyone's hands and the fishing lines in the water. Instead, Mike kept going on and on about the power of the engines and missed this perfect opportunity to close the sale quickly.

After the customer left, I suggested to Mike that he call up the fellow, invite him to meet at the dock of the marina at 5:30 AM on the next Saturday and to bring 2 of his best buddies with him. In a cooler, Mike would bring a six pack or two of beer and enough ham sandwiches to fill a small cooler. He should also bring a sales contract with him because that would be all the customer would need to experience for him to want to buy that boat that day. Mike had a choice. He could sell the boat or he could sell what the customer really wanted, which was his fantasy of the boating experience.

Make sure the words you use include strong emotionally evocative language, designed to make the receiver FEEL something and the deal is done. Legend has it that the movie "Aliens" was sold in a pitch session to studio executives using only 4 words: "JAWS IN OUTER SPACE." That was all that was needed to get the producers to wrap their heads around funding the filming of Sigourney Weaver and her cast of slimy extra-terrestrials.

We live in a "sound bite" society where people are bombarded with too much information. They tend to tune out anything that is too long or complicated. Think of these famous catchphrases:

1) We Try Harder
2) Just Do It
3) Guaranteed Over Night
4) Got Milk?

We don't need to hear too much more to get the message. Everyone knows the organizations behind these messages. Everyone gets the picture. Quickly. The fewer words, the better.

Do you/your organization know how to interest your employees and customers with short, highly emotional messaging? The first tool to consider is the 30-second pitch. Imagine meeting a potential customer in an elevator on the ground floor. You may have 30 seconds of his time in which to plant a seed and cultivate some interest in what you have to offer. It is important to remember that the purpose of the 30-second pitch is not really to sell anyone anything. The real purpose of the 30-second pitch is to get 3 more minutes of their time so you can set your "sales hook" deeper. The purpose of the 3-minute pitch is to get 30 minutes in which you can begin to seal the deal.

What are the 5 components of a great 30-second pitch?

1) Ask a leading question.

   This is designed to lead the listener to the heroin, that key piece of information that you want the person to walk away with.). Usually this is a "Yes" or "No" question that really piques the listener's interest. Samples include:

   a) Are YOU making as much money as YOU want?
   b) Would YOU like to get something valuable for free?
   c) Would YOU like me to let you in on something that few other people know?

   This generally draws the desired answer of "tell me about it" and opens the door for further conversation.

2) Plant the heroin.

   How many of you have ever really sold heroin? Probably not that many. If you had, you are most likely reading this book in prison. Here's all you need to know about selling heroin.

   What do you think the price of the first sample is? Zero. Nothing. Nada. Why is the price zero? To get you interested and then hooked so that the price for continuing heroin will become incredibly expensive.

This step involves usage of the highest level of EMOTIONALLY EVOCATIVE LANGUAGE. What is the most important idea that you can give this person in the most dramatic fashion that will cause this person to understand and empathize with you? Remember one sentence or a phrase can change someone's life if it is said at the right time in the right way by the right person.

3) Speak with passion.

Look, act and sound enthusiastic about your product or idea. Excitement is contagious. If you want someone else to believe in you or your product, you have to "walk the talk." If you say you are really excited about something, you should look like you are excited. This is particularly important for scientists, engineers and financial people. (Note: Some of them may need to rent a personality, before they actually have one, in order to show real excitement.)

(Note: This is not an excuse for hype. Most people are sophisticated enough to have reasonably good BS detectors. If they sense that you are not sincere and real, all of your emotionally evocative language will be perceived as hype and promptly disregarded.)

4) Add more heroin.

If you have time, you can make your product/service even more attractive. Sometimes a second dose is needed. A good test to see if a second dose is needed is to check the body language of the receiver. How did they respond to the first dose? If they are excited already, move on to Step 5. If not, offer them more.

5) Call to Action.

Get them to do something. Get their business card. Offer them your business card. Ask if you can call them or stop by to tell them more. Get an appointment for your 3-minute pitch, which will largely follow this same formula with a bit more depth.

Sounds easy? It isn't. Jerry Seinfeld is noted as one of the most precise comics around. When Jerry crafts a joke, he reads it over many times and asks himself if every word in the joke is needed to get the big laugh at the end. He edits out every word that is not necessary. The difference between a professional comic and an amateur telling the same joke is how many words they have to use to get the laugh.

Are you a pro or not? Imagine if Jerry went through your sales material and asked you to justify every word that you use. What would happen to your communications, if every conversation, presentation and email was subjected to that type of scrutiny and evaluation?

I have sat through too many power point presentations where there were too many words and concepts on each slide. In an effort to provide lots of information and justification, the essence of each slide often gets lost. Imagine if each slide had only one major idea on it and that idea was highlighted using emotionally compelling language so that anyone could get the idea.

One more idea. In "Blink," Malcolm Gladwell writes about "thin slicing." Thin slicing occurs when people respond strongly to their first impressions of another idea or person. Gladwell claims that first impressions are often as enduring and accurate as receiving larger amounts of data. He suggests that by the time a potential employment candidate enters the door and sits down at the HR person's desk to hear the first interview question, both the candidate and the interviewer have already largely decided on whether or not this person is a candidate for a second interview or a good fit for the job.

Applying this knowledge to the dating world dictates that first dates should only be held for only brief durations such as at car washes.

Both parties should bring their vehicles to the car wash. In the time that it takes to run both cars through the wash, wax and rinse cycles, both people will probably have already decided if they ever want to see each other again. Why waste time sitting through a long dinner with those awkward pauses when a car wash would do the trick? At the very least, you end up with a clean car. The less said, the better. But enough about dating.

THOUGHT BOMBS TO PONDER

1) Are you concise when you communicate with others? Or do you cover some of your uncertainty with tons of extra information?
2) Do you have a 30-second pitch about yourself? Your product/ service? Your organization? When was the last time you modified it?
3) Have you reviewed your presentations recently to see if there is too much data contained in them? Have you received feedback from your audience?
4) Are your communications emotionally powerful? Have you considered which words that you use have the most emotional impact?
5) How do you feel using emotionally evocative language? Does it feel "real" to you?

CHAPTER 8

PERSONALIZING YOUR MESSAGES

COMMON SENSE

People don't hear and understand what you are saying till you say it 3-7 times. Keep repeating the message till they get it. KISS them (Keep It Simple Stupid). Be consistent in your messaging. Stay on point. (Whoa, I am getting George Bush flashbacks here.)

UNCOMMON SENSE

OK, people do need to hear the message a few times, BUT not exactly the same message each time. Each person has a different set of hearing aids and other filters that determine what is most meaningful to them. The more you customize the message to the individual, the more likely it will be understood and acted upon.

One of the benefits of technology is that you are just one click away from sending out a message to:

1) everyone on your email list;
2) everyone you have friended on Facebook; or
3) Everyone in your Linked In account.

Common Sense tells us that's great. One click. One message can be sent to the entire world. UnCommon Sense tells us that we pay a high price for this convenience. Will every person on those lists read and interpret the message the same way?

Probably not. Some will like it. Some will pass over it quickly and others will delete it without even reading it. While most of you do not have the luxury of being able to communicate your thoughts to everyone who has to hear them in a one-on-one fashion, think of how much more personal, more meaningful and more powerful YOUR communication could be if it were customized.

In the classic book "Megatrends," John Naisbitt suggests that High Technology needs to be tempered by High Touch. When you communicate at a distance, without seeing the other person or hearing their voice, you need to personalize the message to offset the impersonality of the communication medium.

Here is a tool to help you do this. Start doing this with your most important communications and then decide on a ROIT (Return On Invested Time) basis whether or not to continue. This tool will help you to create "A BOOK" on the people that you communicate with and suggests that you consult that "BOOK" before you talk to, write or email those people.

What is the BOOK? It is a quick set of questions that will help you determine the best way to present your information to that person. It is about being "political" with that person. Now before, you slam this book down and say, "I don't want to be political. There is no way that I want to be a butt kisser, apple polisher, yes man, toad or some other type of phony person," that is not what I mean by being "Political."

The UnCommon Sense definition of "Politics" means presenting ideas WHILE BEING HONEST to other people so that those ideas have the maximum opportunity of being favorably received.

Do you want your ideas to be heard? Do you think that that those ideas might be heard in a different way by people who liked you? Disliked you? Didn't know you? You bet they will! That is why you need to customize your message whenever you can. In order to have a "BOOK" on someone, you should ask and answer AT LEAST the following 13 things about your communication receiver:

1) What does the communication receiver most need and want? (As Bob Dylan once sang, "Your debutantes know what you NEED, BUT I know what you WANT.")

2) What is the receiver most frightened about? What keeps them up at night? What are they trying to avoid?

3) How do they process information? Do they like simple answers? Complex answers? Multiple Options? Evidence? Research? Verbal information? Pictures? Do they like to figure it out for themselves? Do they like it in person? On the phone? By Email? In a Tweet?

4) How do they make decisions once they get that information? Do they mull it over? Make quick impulsive decisions? Check with experts? Consult their horoscope? Check Consumer Reports or other experts? Ask their friends? Flip a coin? Search the Net?

5) Are they more Emotional or Logical?

6) Are they more Introverted (quieter and more likely to keep their thoughts to themselves) or Extroverted (louder and more likely to tell you what they are thinking)?

7) Are they more interested in Tasks? (Getting the Work Done) or Relationships (How Other People Will Feel)?

8) How much education do they have? Schooling? Common Sense? UnCommon Sense?

9) What language do they speak? Technical? Financial? Esoteric? What buzzwords do they use?

10) What is their work background? Are they Designers? Marketers? Customer Service Professionals? Executives? Boots on the Ground Personnel?

11) Who are their Allies? Who are their Enemies? Who do they associate with? Who do they respect? Who do they ignore?

12) What are their personal idiosyncrasies? What is unique about them? What makes them the people that they are?

13) What do they think about you? Your Product? Your Idea? Your organization?

Is that it? Just 13 items? Nope. Anything and everything about this person that matters to you or them should be factored in as well. If their closest companion is a dog named Guster or Watson, you ought to know that as well. Think of all the factors that could impact how your communication will be received. All of that should be included in your BOOK on each customer.

Think of the 3 most important people whom you communicate with on a regular basis. Do you know all of these things about them? Maybe. Think of all the other people you chat with on a regular basis. Do you know all of these things about them? Probably not. So what should you do if you don't know these things about them? Try these methods to help you complete your book:

1) ASK THEM.
2) Ask others who have worked with them before.
3) Observe them carefully when they speak with other people.
4) Float a "trial balloon" in front of them (not the actual idea you want to communicate with them) and see how they react.
5) Check out what they have put into writing.

The more you know about your communication receiver, the easier it is to know how to present ideas to them. In the beginning, it is a good idea to keep an actual "BOOK" where you write this information down. In this way, when you get ready to communicate with them, you can review what you know and craft your message in the most "political" manner. Once you see the power of the "BOOK," you will find that it is to your advantage to memorize as much of this information as possible so that it is readily available to you all of the time.

Consider my dentist, Drew. Drew is a talented dentist who really knows his stuff. He can actually tell you how many teeth you have in your mouth. He has been in practice for over 20 years and has a great chair side manner. You truly get the feeling that he wants to help you to achieve optimal dental health. Unfortunately, the language that he speaks is "Dentese," a language known only to trained dental personnel. There is no "English-Dentese" dictionary available to patients so that they can figure out what the heck he is actually talking about.

In one of my first visits to his office, he set about diagnosing my "dental issues." Candidly, I do not have the best teeth in the world. Years of eating candy and not flossing had left me with enough silver and other precious metals in my mouth to open up a small mining company. While we're on the subject, I contend that flossing your teeth is not a natural activity for humans to do by themselves. It would be much easier for others to floss your teeth than for you to do so. Not that most of us have many people who would volunteer to floss our teeth. But I digress.

For all that Drew knew about me, I don't think he had a "book" on my dental concerns. While some people are concerned about how their smile looks, the presence of mercury in their old fillings and the prospect of not having to "gum their food" in their declining years, my concerns were rather simple. I enjoy having teeth and eating with them. Since I travel on the road quite a bit, I just want to make sure that they stay in working order wherever I am. Sounds simple.

When Drew looked in my mouth and saw my bite wing x-rays, I suspect that he saw lots of payments for his stylish sports car. The first thing he pointed out was that one of my teeth had a small crack in it. Then, he started to list all the crowns that I needed to replace. The total dental bill probably amounted to well over $10K. I don't really remember much about what the total treatment plan was because I stopped listening after he told me about the cracked tooth.

At that point, all I could think about was traveling to do a show somewhere in the middle of Kansas and having my cracked tooth crack completely. There I would be near Salina, Kansas with a broken tooth. Now I am certain that they have some great dentists in Kansas, so I don't need letters from the KDA (Kansas Dental Association), but all I could imagine at this point was a country dentist, wearing overalls yanking out my cracked tooth with a string tied to a doorknob.

My point is that Drew never realized that I had stopped listening to him. He droned on in "Dentese" about which crowns should be done first. He did this in a complete and caring fashion that was entirely lost on me because I could only think about Toto from The Wizard Of Oz and the fact that I was happy I was not in Kansas. Drew made only 4 mistakes:

1) He didn't have a "Book" on me and my dental wants, needs and fears.
2) He didn't check my interest or concentration on what he was saying even once during the presentation.
3) He communicated with me in "Dentese."
4) In his effort to be complete and comprehensive, he gave me so much data that I rushed out of his office in shock without scheduling any treatment.

If he had only asked how I felt about the cracked tooth, I would have had him fix that tooth right then and there at almost any price. Even if I didn't have money to pay for the repair of the tooth, I would have cleaned "spit bowls" for a week just to get the picture of that Kansas dentist yanking my tooth out with a door knob out of my mind.

THOUGHT BOMBS TO PONDER

1) Is your "Book" up to date on the key people you communicate with? Do you consult it before interacting with them? Do you check with them while you are communicating to see if your "Book" is accurate and working?
2) If I asked your customers, vendors and employees what language they think you speak, what would they say?
3) Do you have a "Book" on your employees so that you know how to influence them in the best way?
4) What price are you paying for "one size fits all" communications like blast e-mails and distribution list memos?
5) Do you ever check with people whom you communicate with regularly to make sure they understand what you are trying to tell them?

CHAPTER 9

EMOTIONAL SELLING

COMMON SENSE

Selling is a step-by-step logical process. People buy products because of the price and features of the product. The role of the sales person is minimal.

UNCOMMON SENSE

The salesperson (if they are skilled and talented) can be the most important element of the sales call, assuming that the price and features are relatively similar.

Growing up in the 1960's, I watched many groups put forth radical ideas. Most of the time, those ideas were rejected in the short run. In the long run, some of those ideas eventually did get traction.

Why did this occur? If you look at it logically, many of those ideas were sound in principle. Many of the spokespersons were reasonable individuals. The forums in which they were broadcast were appropriate for the messages, yet the messages often failed to connect with the mainstream. Civil rights groups, equality groups, anti-war groups all thought that their message was crystal clear and that the mainstream would hear the message and make a quantum shift in their beliefs.

That was the problem. Groups do not make quantum shifts in accepting new ideas. They make slow gradual shifts for a variety of reasons, most of them EMOTIONAL, not logical. Albert Einstein's theory of relativity was not immediately accepted. The world was simply not ready for it. Einstein later offered, "Great spirits have always encountered violent opposition from mediocre minds." Einstein didn't realize why his ideas weren't accepted. His peers weren't necessarily mediocre; it just took them a while to find other data to substantiate his claims.

Here are a few of the reasons that people don't change their minds in quantum leaps:

1) Accepting a new idea requires you to "unfreeze" old ideas that can be deeply embedded. It may involve admitting that you were wrong or behaved foolishly in the past. This admission is tough on the ego. Admitting that you were wrong is not very palatable to certain individuals.

2) Accepting a new idea may involve changing other ideas that are connected to the new idea. This means that you are not only changing one thought pattern; you must now consider related issues as well. People seek consistency in their thinking. It is significantly easier to throw out one new thought as opposed to having to reorganize a series of related thoughts.

3) Fear begins to creep in when new ideas are accepted. You begin to think, "If I was wrong about this idea, maybe I have been wrong about other ideas." Fear can be viewed as an attack on the system, as a whole, resulting in the use of psychological defenses such as rationalization, intellectualization and compensation.

4) There is a natural distrust of zealots. You have seen your share of false prophets who routinely make claims that seem terrific on the surface. Upon closer inspection, their claims do not stand up. Although society seeks easy, painless answers to complex problems, complex problems usually demand complex answers.

Consider the last time when you had a "great idea" and went to your boss/department with your flash of genius only to be summarily denied. It didn't feel great and you probably hatched schemes to bring about the hasty and evil demise of your boss. You probably didn't consider the notion that perhaps the shortcoming was in the manner in which you attempted to "sell" the idea.

One of the major premises of this book is that people buy ideas emotionally and then justify their emotional purchases with logic. Here is an UnCommon Sense model to use when "selling" your ideas to a group/individual.

A FIVE-STEP MODEL FOR EMOTIONAL SELLING

Emotional selling involves the following 5 steps:

1) Creating awareness/planting seeds
2) Sizing the gap/knowing how much to sell at one time
3) Presenting the benefits to the user, not just the features of the idea
4) SELLING THE SIZZLE
5) Driving action

This model can be used to sell products, services or ideas. These steps do not necessarily have to be done in order. At times, it may be necessary to backtrack and repeat several of the steps. The most critical point about this model is that it doesn't work well (or at all) unless you do a terrific job on Step #4. SELLING THE SIZZLE is where the emotional connection is made. It is also where the sale is made. Here is what is involved during each step:

CREATING AWARENESS/PLANTING SEEDS

Too often when a person has a "great idea," they want to present it in one fell swoop, --lock, stock and barrel. They expect that when other people hear the idea, they will also be ready to make a quantum leap and accept it.

Think of the last encounter that you had with a religious zealot. They were so excited about "having found God" that they wanted to immediately share it with you. They wanted you to become as excited as they were and join them in their quest. I suspect that many of them are truly shocked when they are repeatedly rejected.

People are more likely to buy your new ideas when they have had some exposure to the idea prior to your "sales call." They usually need 3-7 repetitions of the idea before it begins to sound familiar to them. These repetitions are not necessarily rote repetitions. More likely they are variations on a theme. Imagine if during every conversation, phone call, presentation or meeting, you were able to deal with the business at hand AND also plant a "seed" about possible future ideas. Intentionally placing ideas in front of others according to your "book" on them can smooth the way for your sales call.

There are two kinds of seeds that can planted: seeds of hope and seeds of doubt. Seeds of hope illustrate positive possibilities that could occur; seeds of doubt suggest negative consequences. It is important to mention that fear messages are quite strong in small doses. The less often you use fear, the stronger the impact. The constant and repeated use of fear messages dulls their impact. Nancy Reagan's oft repeated mantra of "Just say No to drugs" was the object of ridicule in the 1980's and probably resulted in increased awareness and an increased usage of drugs. The impact of the message had been lost.

Planting seeds is not enough. If you have ever tried to grow a vegetable garden, you know it is not enough to throw a seed into the ground and then expect to see a vegetable appear 70 days later. Think of all the steps involved.

1) The ground must be prepared.
2) A growing medium must be put in place so the seed can receive nourishment.
3) The seeds must be spread out so they don't compete with one another.
4) The seed must receive adequate sunlight, water and fertilizer.
5) Weeds must be quickly pulled.
6) The weather must be cooperative.
7) Pests and plant eaters must be kept at bay.

If all of these activities are accomplished, a tomato may grow and be viable to eat in 2 months or so. Think of all that you must do to keep your seeds on the front page of your decision makers. Too many people selling ideas are in a rush to deliver the idea and harvest the results immediately. As my martial arts teacher, Rey, used to say, "Don't be in a rush to go nowhere."

SIZING THE GAP/KNOWING HOW MUCH TO SELL AT ONE TIME

Consider the idea that you want to sell. The more radical your idea is to your decision makers, the more care you will have to apply at this step. Look at the bell shaped curve below:

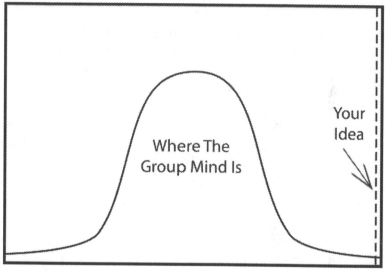

Diagram 1

If your idea is 2-3 standard deviations from the norm, you must realize what will happen if your idea is presented as a totality. Typically, three things will occur:

1) People in the mainstream who may be favorable to your idea begin to listen more carefully and begin to accept easily digestible parts of your idea. They begin to shift in the direction of your idea.

2) People in the mainstream who are not favorable to your idea begin to reject your idea and begin to shift in the opposite

direction. They potentially feel uncomfortable and attacked by the idea and therefore begin to use psychological defenses to fend off the idea.

(Note: Common Sense deems this to be a negative reaction. In the short run, it may well be negative. UnCommon Sense suggests that in the long run, groups that consider the widest possible array of options often make the best decisions. When groups polarize within the mainstream, it allows exposure to new and radical ideas. Even though those ideas may not be immediately accepted, they become part of the long term conversation. (Think of the Tea Party rhetoric in that context.)

3) Your ideas are rejected because:
   a) You can't gain consensus within the group.
   b) You are viewed as a polarizer.
   c) You are viewed as too radical for your time.

I have a colleague who has always been a man before his time. He seemed to have a crystal ball that allowed him to see the future of technology and opportunity before others. Being a pioneer in the world of satellite communications, Ed enjoyed keeping his ear to the ground. He was well read, and his quick mind could grasp the possibilities long before the mainstream.

Working with a major pay television provider, he was responsible for one of the first uplinks of signals to satellites hovering over the globe. He envisioned an 18" satellite receiver dish, while the world was still locked into 3-foot diameter dishes. Imagine having a 3-foot dish mounted on the roof of your house today. However, the company was not quite ready for the rush into the technological future. Ed became frustrated and began to seek new opportunities.

He later landed with a major global bank to help launch electronic banking options. The plan for the bank was ambitious. It called for the bank to become "one mile, one click or one call from 80% of the people who use banking services on the PLANET." Quite imaginative. It involved considering using biometrics to replace ATM cards and PIN numbers. One small problem. Once the bank merged with another conglomerate, a power struggle ensued between the two CEO's. The CEO who eventually triumphed believed that the "internet was just a fad" and refused to fund further technological advances.

Again, Ed moved on seeking not to have to deal with Einstein's "mediocre minds." Perhaps instead the problem was the far reaching implications of Ed's vision. Perhaps Ed just expected people to grasp too much too quickly.

Is there a little bit of Ed in you? Are you in a rush to gather support for your ideas? If so, what options do you have?

Throughout this book, I have encouraged you to be bold and consider when to break precedent. It is one of the elements that sets UnCommon Sense apart from Common Sense.

Here is the UnCommon Sense answer. When you realize that your idea may be disruptive, it is important to use your "BOOK" on your decision makers. Consider how much change they can tolerate at one time. Review how long it took in the past. Review their decision-making style and determine what caused them to change their minds previously. The critical concept is to break your idea into smaller chunks. Make sure that the first idea you present is close enough to the mainstream to:

1) engender support from sympathizers
2) not engender a strong fear reaction from potential rejecters
3) not result in getting you labeled as too radical.

See the diagram below:

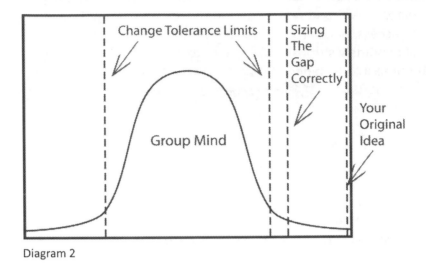

Diagram 2

To be successful when you have radical ideas, it is important not to be perceived as a radical. There are only 2 rules here:

1) Rule #1 is to keep your job.
2) Rule #2 is to remember Rule #1.

PRESENTING THE BENEFITS, NOT JUST THE FEATURES

Recognize that everyone listens to basically one radio station: WIIFM (What's In It for Me.) You would be better off by broadcasting from WIIFY (What's In It for You), the sister station. Too often sales people become enamored with the features of the idea/product or service that they offer. Since they are knowledgeable about the idea/product/service, being able to highlight all the features gives the sales person the opportunity to show off their extensive knowledge. That works for the sales person. It doesn't work so well for the user. If the salesperson can't put themselves into the shoes of the user, they may highlight features that are not relevant to the user.

Many years ago, I went to buy a cell phone. I am not always an early adopter when it comes to new technology. I went over and started to look at the phone display, and a young sales person immediately glommed onto me and began telling me about the "latest and greatest" features of the newest phones. He started to talk about web access, photo capabilities and new apps. I had to stop him. He was genuinely surprised because he had barely begun to tell me all of the fabulous things that the phone could do.

I reminded him that my basic need was for a phone that could "take calls and make calls." At that time I did not use my phone to surf the web, take pictures or order books from Amazon. He stepped backward and must have wondered how a caveman could have found his way to the store. When he heard that, he simply said in a disgusted voice, "All of them do that. Why don't you pick out the one you like?" He then left me to find a more knowledgeable customer to work with.

Great sales people have the ability to morph into their customers. They can instantly see the world through the customer's eyes and know what the customer perceives as a benefit. Presenting features that the customer doesn't value is wasting everyone's time. Presenting features that the customer values is a different story. Presenting benefits helps to "seal the deal."

SELL THE SIZZLE

The first 3 steps set the sales person up to "seal the deal." Ultimately, the first three steps get the decision maker interested, but the sizzle is the clincher.

y favorite example of how to turn a loser of a product into a winner is the soft drink Mountain Dew. I would love to have been a fly on the wall at the original pitch session for Mountain Dew. The original formula was invented in 1940 by Tennessee bottlers Barney and Ally Hartman. It was first marketed in Virginia and Tennessee with the slogan: "Ya-Hoo, Mountain Dew. It'll tickle your innards." Now if the product was destined only for regional distribution to Appalachia and other rural areas, it would have been fine. However, when the product was initially set for national distribution, it was not a hit. There were several significant issues standing in the way:

1) The name Mountain Dew was not likely to connect with urban dwellers. The hillbilly twang used in the advertisement would turn off anyone who considered themselves to be urbane and sophisticated.

2) The color of the Dew was quite unique. When I look at the bright green liquid, it reminds of the only 2 other products that I know that come in that shade: antifreeze and a variety of hazmat substances (none of which you would be tempted to drink).

3) The colors in the advertising sent conflicting messages. Without going deeply into color associations in advertising, red and green send contradictory messages. Traffic lights use red and green to signify different activities. There was no accident in deciding to use those colors. Traffic lights with blue, orange and brown lights would not have been as effective. No disrespect intended to countries whose flags are red, green and white. Advertising is a different story and the color combination was odd at best.

In summary, the product name was regionalized, the product color was off putting and the advertising colors sent confusing signals. On top of that the product had NO SIZZLE to the majority of the target audience. which did not necessarily want its innards tickled. The product was not considered a major soft drink brand and failed to deliver on its promise.

In 1964, a company that understands SIZZLE purchased Mountain Dew and added it to its bouquet of products. Pepsi Cola clearly understood that it would have to overcome huge hurdles in order to gain market share. Curiously, they kept the product name, the product color (although they added other colors later) and the colors in the advertising (although they changed the shade of green and made it darker). So what did they do? To begin to understand SIZZLE, it is essential to understand the demographics of your customer base.

What kind of people would be drawn to a beverage that had enough caffeine and sugar to power up a small town? The answer is straight forward. The Dew was largely consumed by young adolescent boys who loved the extra energy provided by the Dew. For me, if I drank a large Mountain Dew tonight, I would be lucky to get to sleep 2 days from now.

If you began watching the advertising for the Dew, it also underwent a major change. Pepsi understood that the target segment of the population is strongly attracted to extreme sports. Early ads connected the Dew to extreme sports. Commercials showing a teenager schussing down the side of a mountain in a recliner screaming in joy were accompanied by the simple yet effective tag line of "Do the Dew." The more extreme the sports, the higher the market share. Users somehow connected drinking the Dew with the courage/bravado attached to extreme sports. The Dew became associated with the "X" games, the Olympics for extreme sports. More recent ads took the Dew to another level when young girls seemed to be attracted to boys who were drinking the Dew. The subliminal message was "Do the Dew and maybe she'll do YOU." Now that's SIZZLE.

SIZZLE is all about appealing to the decision maker at a core emotional level using emotionally evocative language. It allows the decision maker to associate themselves with the idea/product/service at a feeling level. SIZZLE means different things to different people. To teenagers, SIZZLE evokes thoughts and feelings about popularity, sexuality and staying current in terms of technology, fashion, music and media. It uses current idioms. I am constantly reminded by my daughter that when I used the expression "that was so five minutes ago," I am dating myself to a time in ancient history. When I wear my "Members Only" jacket, she reminds me that I must be the last remaining member.

To an older generation, SIZZLE evokes thoughts and feelings about safety, having arrived, prudence, security and sexuality at times (the ads for Viagra and Cialis come to mind.) SIZZLE is all about what makes a person feel great.

Once the decision maker has associated the product with the feeling engendered by SIZZLE, they will seek to find logic to justify their decision to buy the idea/product/ service. For all intents and purposes, the deal is closed the moment this happens. Skilled sales people will seek to inject SIZZLE as early into the sales call as they can.

DRIVING ACTION

Everything that you have done to this point is designed to get the decision maker to sign on the dotted line. It doesn't do any good to have invested all of this time and energy into the sales process to end up with an "I'm going to sleep on it" of "I'll get back to you. Henny Youngman put it well when he said, "Get the Check." He wasn't satisfied to "Get the Contract." He wanted the check. Why? A contract may mean 10 cents on the dollar after the issue is litigated in court ten years from now. The check can be deposited today.

Some sales people seem to be afraid to ask for the signature. They feel that by being "pushy" at the end, they run the risk of losing the sale. I think we have generated a bunch of "order takers" as opposed to sales people. Order takers want the decision maker to step up and close the deal him/herself. If you have done all of the groundwork correctly, there is no reason to be ashamed to ask for the signature.

As a reminder, "selling" is "helping" the individual reach for their dreams. When the deal is closed, you have helped the individual accomplish what THEY WANT. No reason to be reluctant or timid here.

When I "sell" ideas, I talk about closing the deal early in the conversation. Many sales gurus have said, "Closing starts with the word HELLO." A great sales person is constantly looking for closing cues. The earlier it occurs, the better for all involved. Some sales people are so process driven that they miss early closing cues. They are focused on delivering their full presentation, identifying and overcoming obstacles and then moving in for the close. It is as if they are so proud of their process and the opportunity it provides for them to show how smart they are. Get the check and move on. The more you sell, the smarter you are.

Closing cues are easy to spot when you are looking for them. The tone of questions start shifting from "Why should I buy this?" to "How can I use this?" and "When can I get it?" The decision maker's body language switches from adversarial to collaborative. The arms uncross. The posture is more open. The person moves toward you. They relax. Watching their eyes can tell you quite a bit here. Once their eyes start to move upward, the decision maker is often imagining how the idea/product/service will work.

How good are you at spotting these clues?

THOUGHT BOMBS TO PONDER:

1) Are you Johnny or Janey Apple Seed, constantly planting seeds during your conversations with others? Do you fertilize those seeds? Do you plant more seeds of hope or more seeds of doubt?

2) Are your ideas too radical or have you right sized them according to your "book" on your receivers? Remember there is little value in presenting ideas that are too much for your receivers to accept.

3) Are you presenting more features or benefits to your customer? Do you have the need to show them how smart you are?

4) Are you a SIZZLER? Can you present ideas using emotionally evocative language that get to the heart of the matter and to the heart of your customer?

5) Can you get the check? Are you shy about asking your customer to sign on the dotted line?

CHAPTER 10

TELLING VS. SELLING

COMMON SENSE

People don't like or respect sales people because they feel like the sales people are stretching the truth (read *lying like bandits*) or taking advantage of them. They feel like they are being hustled into buying products or ideas that they don't want or need.

UNCOMMON SENSE

Every person is selling most of the time. We all sell different services or ideas at different prices, but we are all in the sales business. It is important to educate and persuade others about products and ideas that they don't know enough about. As long as we are honest and ethical, we can help bring light to the world and co-create a better future.

Do you define your job as a "sales" job? Most people don't like the word "selling" because it conjures up visions of greasy, slimy used car sales people and door-to-door "tin men" selling aluminum siding for your home. The old joke goes, "How do you know if a salesman is lying?" "His lips are moving." Professional people are even more reticent about "selling" anything to anyone. The implication is that when you are an expert about something, you should not have to "sell" your ideas. Your expertise should be reason enough for people to believe you and do as you suggest. Doctors and dentists are notoriously poor salespeople because they believe patients should simply do what is advised. They believe that all they have to do is tell the patient what to do.

In the first year of my job as a cable television door-to-door salesman, I constantly denied that I was a salesman. To anyone who would listen, I would explain that I was a poor graduate student, simply offering cable television to the citizens of NYC to help me pay my tuition. Not only did I take no pride in my profession, I was embarrassed by it. I did not want people lumping me into the category with "those other sales people." How silly.

The concept of selling has gotten a bum rap. Would people be so disgusted with selling if they thought about it in terms of "helping" or "providing a service" to others? Those are more useful ways in which to view selling.

Think of what you are doing when you authentically sell a product or idea that you believe in. You are providing help or a needed service to someone who will be happy to have that product or service. There are lots of ways to sell -- from the high-powered, arm twisting ploys of timeshare vacation sales people to the more elegant soft-sell approaches of a skilled sales manager in a plastic surgeon's office and everything in between.

Let's take a closer look at a few critical differences between telling and selling an employee or customer:

TELLING	SELLING
1. Focus is on the data.	Focus is on the employee/customer.
2. Knowledge of the task/product is what matters most.	Knowledge of the person (BOOK) is what matters most.
3. Logic drives the presentation.	Emotion drives the presentation.
4. Presenter/leader speaks more.	Customer/employee speaks more.
5. Tells, Tells Louder, Tells Even Louder	Asks, Sells, Tells
6. Presents data as prepared.	Modifies presentation to fit the customer/employee.

When you are the customer, how would you like to be treated?

Which style is most appealing to you?

Which of these styles best describes how you deal your customers/employees?

Which style encourages you to read your customer/employee and react?

Consider this sales call by Javier:

I was watching sales personnel for a fishing boat company trying to sell their wares at the biggest boat show in the world, held annually in Miami, Florida. Javier was one of the best sales guys at the show. He positioned himself on the deck of one of the top-of-the-line boats, selling for almost a half million dollars (delivered with all of the electronic goodies that a fisherman could imagine.) The boat was beautiful, and Javier knew everything there was to know about the boat.

A couple came to see the boat, and Javier quickly separated the man from his wife. He proceeded to talk "boats" with the husband. He chatted with him for a good 20 minutes, showing him every nook and cranny of the vessel. His wife was left alone.

Seeing this, I asked his wife a few questions. The first thing I did was ask her name, which was Yolanda. Next I asked her about her boating experiences and what was important to her about any boat they might buy. She mentioned her concerns about being on a boat where every sound and smell made themselves known. She also said that, since they would probably be entertaining friends on the boat, she wanted a kitchen that would be easy to spend time in and had enough storage to keep things looking clean. Additionally, she spoke about how she looked forward to long quiet weekends with Javier docked in Biscayne Bay.

Armed with that knowledge, I offered to show Yolanda a few things that I thought she might appreciate about this particular boat. I asked her if she had ever used the bathroom on a boat. She smiled when I suggested to her that she might actually be willing to use the bathroom on this boat because all of the sounds and smells that would typically emanate from most boats were muffled and then vented. I asked her to go into the bathroom, close the door and waited for her to come out. She smiled again and said that this was the first boat that she had ever been on which was designed to deal with sensitivities and concerns such as hers.

I then talked to Yolanda about the kitchen and storage area. We chatted about how easy it would be to entertain on the boat because of the spacious design.

Finally, I suggested that she lie down on the bed in the master suite and gaze out through the sky light and imagine the peaceful sounds of the ocean with the beams of light from a full moon pouring in as she finished her day next to her husband. I watched the smile fill her face as she imagined a carefree weekend off the Florida coast.

Javier finished chatting with the husband, Octavio, and NEVER SAID ONE WORD to Yolanda. After the couple left, I asked Javier if he knew whether or not Octavio was married. He looked at me with the look that said, "Why should I care about that?" I reminded Javier that Octavio was not going to be able to buy that boat, if Yolanda, his wife, didn't agree and like the boat as well.

I asked Javier if he knew what concerns Yolanda might have about buying the boat. He thought about it and then said, "All she probably cares about is the kitchen." I told him that he was correct on 1 of the 3 things that mattered to Yolanda. Javier started to grow uneasy and realized that his "in-the-bag" sale to Octavio might require an apology to Yolanda and more attention to her needs and wants. Javier spent so much time impressing Octavio with his boat knowledge that he barely spent any time thinking about what Octavio's family would want and need. Clearly, selling is much more about asking questions than telling.

Another critical point about selling is that the best sales personnel use questions to control the conversation. Most sales people try to control the sales call by constant chatter. They believe that, if they keep on talking, the customer will not be able to raise too many objections. However, great salespeople are so skilled that they only need to speak 1/3 of the time, leaving the other 2/3 of the time for the customer to speak. If the salesperson, develops strong rapport with the customer, uses emotionally evocative language and is a great listener, he/she won't need to speak more than 1/3 of the time.

Consider what you can discover about your customer or employee by using UnCommon Sense to ask the right questions:

1) Establish rapport.
2) Show your listening and empathy skills.
3) Discover "Book" information.
4) Discover problems or stumbling blocks.
5) Isolate objections.
6) Answer objections.
7) Build mini-agreements.
8) Amplify the emotional "heroin."
9) Raise new issues.
10) Give yourself time to think and assess what is going on.
11) Identify where the customer is in the buying cycle.
12) Get unstuck when the sales call bogs down.
13) Most importantly, close the deal.

Ask the right questions and THEN KEEP YOUR MOUTH SHUT so that you can *hear* what the customer is saying.

Although the previous example was about selling a product to a customer, the same approach could be used in selling ideas to your employees.Many leaders feel that leadership is based on what a leader says (tells). UnCommon Sense dictates that leadership is more about asking the right questions and leading people to find their own answers to those questions and then blending those answers into a cohesive vision.

Think of Dr. Martin Luther King's famous "I Have a Dream" speech. Was he the only one who had that dream? Of course not. He simply articulated what was in the hearts and on the minds of millions of other people in the country. An interesting sidebar to that speech was that Dr. King did not originally have the "I Have a Dream" section scripted. It was more so a spontaneous recall of a previous speech prompted by one of the people next to him as he spoke. What a great use of spontaneous emotionally evocative language!

Consider the difference between mission and vision statements written solely by executive leadership as opposed to those that were developed based on employee input. In most organizations today, corporate walls are filled with mission and vision statements that all sound vaguely familiar and fairly similar (as if they were taken directly from the book of mission and vision statements.) When you ask employees if they know what their organization's mission and vision are and more importantly, whether or not the mission and vision statements guide their everyday behavior, you often get a blank look in return.

UnCommon Sense tells us that if we want buy in from our employees, we need to get them to buy in right from the start. Get their input early, use it and craft a goal that works for the majority of the group. Then keep asking questions. The more you ask the right questions, the less you have to tell or sell.

THOUGHT BOMBS TO PONDER

1) When you are trying to influence another person, what percentage of the time do you spend "telling" them what you think?
2) How many questions do you ask to calibrate their understanding, interest and buy in to what you saying? How many questions do you prepare in advance to make sure that you cover all the bases?
3) What is your attitude about "selling?" Do you look forward to those aspects of your job?

4) What is so comfortable about "telling? What is so uncomfortable about "selling?"

5) Have you ever received training to help you sell yourself, your product/service and your organization? Have you ever been recorded while selling so that you could see what you look like during a sales call?

CHAPTER 11

HOW MANY SALES PITCHES DO YOU NEED?

COMMON SENSE

The BEST sales people quickly find the "BEST" pitch that works for them and then use that pitch over and over again. There is little to no need to search for more ways to sell, once you have found the BEST pitch.

UNCOMMON SENSE

There is NO BEST pitch. No matter how glib you are, you will need many pitches to sell many different customers.

The worst thing that can happen to you as a salesperson of products or ideas is to actually make a lot of sales right away. That will give you the false notion that "selling" is easy. It will convince you that your sales pitch is "great." If selling is too easy, it is more likely to be considered "order taking." Every salesperson ought to take a shot at selling something door to door. The tougher the product, the better.

I have very high regard for salespeople who have sold any of the following:

1) Brushes
2) Beauty Supplies
3) Amway products
4) Encyclopedias
5) Newspapers
6) Even Girl Scout cookies

The reason for my high regard is that, as a door-to-door sales person, you get told "No" a lot more times than you get told "Yes." You quickly learn that the script you were given during your sales training may or may not work. If you were clever, you learned how to size up your customers on sight (developed your "Book") and then crafted a unique sales pitch on the spot. Door-to-door selling taught me a lot of UnCommon Sense:

1) People buy products/ideas for emotional reasons and then justify their purchases with logical reasons.
2) People buy products/ideas from people that they like.
3) People buy products/ideas from people that they think like them.
4) People buy products/ideas from people that they think are just like them (the chameleon principle).
5) People prefer to "sell themselves" on products/ideas, rather than feel like they are being sold.
6) People buy products/ideas that SIZZLE.

My favorite sales study suggests that:

44% of all salespeople give up after the first No.

22% of all salespeople give up after the second No.

10-12% of all salespeople give up after the third No.

8-10% of all salespeople give up after the fourth No.

For those of you without a lightning quick mathematical mind or a calculator, that leaves slightly more than 10% of the sales force out there who believe that they can still sell the customer after the customer has SAID NO 4 times. They brought Plan "E" with them. Forget about Plans A and B. Or Even Plans C and D. They brought Plan E. A fifth option.

Too many salespeople today want to be order takers. Keep in mind that selling doesn't even begin until the person has said NO. Until then you *are* an order taker. To a great salesperson, the word NO means MAYBE. MAYBE means YES. So NO is the first step on the road to YES. Sadly, too many people fear the prospect of rejection and give up easily when faced with "nos."

When I first started out selling cable television door to door in the tenements of NYC in 1970, I soon realized that I would need to use "Magic Words," words that immediately resonate emotionally with the potential customer, in order to get them to open up their doors and listen to my pitch.

The ultimate "Magic Word" is FREE. However, depending on the product /service/idea, other potential "Magic Words" are TOP OF THE LINE, LEADING EDGE, LATEST AND GREATEST, SAFEST, MOST RELIABLE, HIGH RESALE VALUE, EXTREMELY ECONOMICAL, etc.

My partner Marty and I started selling cable television. At that time there were 5 free channels on the air. Who could ask for anything more? The idea of paying to watch television was new and dicey at best. Cable television meant a clearer picture, fewer ghosts on the air, and not constantly having to adjust rabbit ears to fine tune your reception. The prospect of being able to watch the NY Knickerbocker basketball games and the NY Ranger hockey games in your own home were also main selling points.

Our door opener involved the "Magic Word" FREE as in FREE installation and FREE for the first month. At times it wasn't free, but, if they were willing to try it out in their homes, we could simply pay their $6 for them for the first month of service. (Our commission was higher than $6 per sale, so it was worthwhile for us to "treat" them to a month of service for FREE.) We thought, "How could anyone turn down FREE?"

We were always mystified that we couldn't sign everyone in NYC up for cable television. (If you'll recall, I previously stated that Book Smarts tell us that there is no FREE lunch.) However, in this case, there was FREE cable TV (for at least 1 month).

Everyone asked what the "catch" was. We simply stated that the customer had to call the company to have the cable removed if they were not satisfied with the service. They also had to arrange for a pickup of the converter box that was placed in their home. Not that much of a catch.

When Marty and I worked together in a building, we always sold on adjacent floors for safety reasons so that we could keep track of one another. We could hear each other knocking on apartment doors and attempting to engage skeptical New Yorkers to talk to us. Sometimes, we could see people silently look out of their peepholes to see if we were legitimate.

NYC was a melting pot city with people from every nation, religion, culture and nationality. Doors often had 3 or more dead bolt locks on them in the buildings that we worked. Unfortunately, our sale brochures were only printed in two languages: English and Spanish. Being NYC salesmen, the fact that neither of us actually spoke any Spanish was considered only a minor hindrance. It never stopped us from trying to promote and sell cable television in every building north of 86th Street.

Marty's behavior with Spanish speakers never ceased to amaze and amuse me. As soon as he sensed movement behind any door, he would quickly say in a loud and confident voice: "Cable Television Here." If the person on the other side of the door said anything like "No habla English," the correct protocol was to slide a Spanish brochure under the door hoping that the person might look at the brochure and become interested. Marty had a slightly different, more NY centric approach to the situation.

He would immediately do 3 things differently:

1) Speak more slowly.
2) Speak more loudly.
3) Add the suffix "ee" to the end of many words hoping that his words would suddenly transcend the language barrier.

I would hear him yell out, "Do youee wantee to buyee cable (pronounced koblay) telebision (sic)," followed by the "MAGIC

WORDS." This included a few words in Spanish such as "Installation GRATIS" or "Uno Montho GRATIS." He had learned that GRATIS meant FREE in Spanish and was determined to cinch the deal with his newly found mastery of the Spanish language.

Ironically, this strange tactic worked sometimes, thereby reinforcing Marty's belief that he had a good pitch. However, there were many times when this approach was unsuccessful. Of course this did not stop him. On certain hot summer nights, after the 20th time of hearing about GRATIS and Koblay television, I would scream down/ up to him, "They aren't deaf. They just don't speak our language."

The point is that one size definitely does not fit all customers. The best sale personnel I have ever met view each potential customer as unique, are able to size them up and then take their best shot. Each sales opportunity is viewed as precious. The salesperson truly enjoys the selling process and the prospect of "helping" someone attain their goal.

I had the good fortune/misfortune to be hired by many banks and credit unions during the 1990's to present my program entitled "The Art of Selling" to their employees. At that time, it was the goal of almost every financial institution to become more sales oriented. I was delighted with the opportunity but quickly saw several stumbling blocks:

1) Bankers were used to saying "NO" to their customers. I don't know if they liked doing that or not, but turning people down for loans, credit, mortgages, etc. was often part of their job. They were not thrilled about having customers say "NO" to them.
2) Bankers were used to sitting in the comfort of their own offices. They rarely were asked to "hit the bricks" and make cold/lukewarm sales calls outside the bank.
3) Most bankers were "one trick ponies" and felt most comfortable offering the products available rather than creatively constructing products for customers in a very competitive marketplace.

My initial approach was to get the bankers to get comfortable with the word "NO." Using SSPS (Successful Sequential Problem Solving (aka 3 success in a row)), I created a sales contest where the first winners were the ones who were the most successful in getting the most "NO's" on their cold calls. This provided an interesting twist. They had to understand and reframe the idea that hearing the word "NO" was not a sign of failure.

The second activity was concerned with getting feedback from potential customers as to why they were saying "No." In this way, "NO" became an essential part of every day., something to learn from and value rather than something to disdain. After all, the best closers in the world close only a quarter to a third of the deals they work on. That means they hear 3 or 4 "NO's for every "Yes." Still, they are considered studs and superstars.

There was a look of terror on the faces of several bankers when I told them that they would have to use a briefcase, pack it with sales material and then "hit the bricks" and go off to meet business people in the neighborhood. The very idea of prospecting was a complete shock to them. They had been so used to waiting for their potential customers to come into the branch that the idea of meeting the customer where they worked was beyond their worst nightmare. Eventually, with a bit of encouragement and practice, they became as comfortable outside their office as they were inside.

I fully believe that more deals today are consummated on golf courses, in restaurants and bars, locker rooms and on tennis courts than in offices. Sales people need to feel comfortable wherever they are. When I get on a Southwest Airlines flight (with their notorious cattle call open seating policy), I quickly survey the open seats and quickly calculate who might be my next prospect. If I assess the situation correctly, I will now have an hour or more of that person's undivided attention as I create my "BOOK" on them and then offer Plans A through E.

In case you are wondering, I love the 5th option. How about you?

THOUGHT BOMBS TO PONDER

1) How many sales approaches do you have? Are you a one trick pony? Do you crave the opportunity to find a new way to seal the deal? Remember that each day is filled with new opportunities to present your products/services/ideas in a unique and creative manner.

2) After 4 "No's" in a row, are you still excited and confident that you can seal the deal? Did you bring Plan "E", the fifth option?

3) What magic words do you typically use? What other magic words could you try?

4) Are you a sales "Chameleon" who can instantly adjust to every customer. Remember that chameleons are green in the grass. They are brown when they are on trees. What is critical is that they don't care whether they are green or brown. They just want to blend in.

5) Do you LOVE the word NO? Do you truly believe that it is the first step on the road to YES?

CHAPTER 12

IS CUSTOMER SERVICE ENOUGH?

COMMON SENSE

Every business must meet their customer's needs if they are to stay in business. Better organizations strive to exceed their customer's needs. We must put the customer at the top of the organization and realize that everyone works for the customer.

UNCOMMON SENSE

Customer's expectations are increasing every day because there is always someone else out there who is working harder than you are to satisfy your customer. Customers are no longer excited with small gestures unless they are heart felt. Customers will continue to expect more and more. Now the best organizations seek to exceed needs, anticipate next needs and provide POM (Peace of Mind.)

We live in a world with escalating expectations. What was once good enough no longer distinguishes you from the rest.

Here is an example:

I had the great privilege and opportunity to make a presentation to the manufacturers, owners and operators of some of the largest limousine companies in the world. The event was held at a prestigious hotel in Las Vegas. My presentation was entitled "Top of the Line Customer Service: What Separates the BEST from the Rest."

The front row consisted of men with very thick necks. Most of them could not turn their heads around to see people in back of them without turning their entire torsos around. They were all of similar ethnicity.

I opened up the presentation by asking what sounded like a simple, straightforward question, "What business are you in?" Quickly one of the men with the thick necks responded in a gruff voice, "The chauffeured transportation business." I acknowledged that he was correct, but I said I was looking for more than that. Another fellow suggested that they were in the "customer service business." I said they were getting closer but that there was another level they had not yet reached. No more suggestions were forthcoming from the 600 people in the audience.

I repeated the question and then said, "You are all in the POM business." POM stands for Peace of Mind. First of all, there is nothing unique about the limousine industry. The vehicles may be spectacular inside and out, but they simply provide a way to get from here to there and back. Most of the special touches inside the vehicle are noticed by customers. But they are not what separate the best from the rest.

Shortly before my presentation, I visited the showroom where the latest and greatest in limousines were on display. There were state-of-the-art sound and music systems, lighting systems and food and beverage systems available. One limousine bus had a stripper pole in the rear. One other vehicle had a Jacuzzi tub. Now I confess that I am not a frequent user of limousine services, so it is not fair for me to judge what others might desire during a limousine ride. I also like to use a Jacuzzi periodically. I might like to use a Jacuzzi before I went somewhere or perhaps after I arrived somewhere. I just have never had the urge/need to use a Jacuzzi WHILE I was going somewhere. But I digress. Thousands of dollars were spent upgrading the limousine experience. However, the was one small problem.

Many of the drivers of these vehicles were making $12 to $15 an hour and had not been trained in anything beyond the simplest elements of customer service:

1) appropriate attire
2) the ability to point out and demonstrate all of the features of the vehicle
3) the ability to drive safely to the appointed destination
4) the value of courtesy and politeness to the passengers
5) knowing when to "look the other way" or "rolling up the dividing glass between driver's compartment and passenger compartment."

You get the idea. But is this POM?

Consider what POM means to different customers. Here is an array of potential different customers for limousine operators:

1) a group of teenagers going to their Senior Prom
2) a business man on the way to the airport
3) a honeymoon couple headed to an exotic location after their wedding
4) several couples going on a wine tasting tour of Napa
5) a group of people gathered for a bachelor or bachelorette party.

Think of what would constitute POM for each of these different customers. In some cases, customers expect complete privacy, minimal conversation and prompt service. To other customers, turning a blind eye to indiscrete behaviors in the back of the vehicle would be most appreciated. To others, being safe, knowledgeable and helpful will do the trick. Each customer will expect the driver to know and display the behavior that THEY expect. A regular $12 to $15 dollar an hour driver may treat all customers the same. That would not result in POM for the majority of his customers. If you are paying top dollar for a first class experience, you expect a first class vehicle AND a first class driver. Many of the limousine companies put a lot more of their attention to the vehicles than to training their drivers.

The key point here is that almost every company is now in the POM business. That is the new standard for expectations. Customers want to buy products and services and then not have to think or worry about them. They want to buy peace of mind knowing that the product or service will do what is expected for a long period of time without additional concern. They also want the highest standard of service.

What level of service are you currently offering? Are you putting more of your attention into the product than into the sales person or service person delivering or explaining the product? Have you trained all of your people to deliver POM service? The standard used to be the golden rule: "Do unto others as you would have others do unto you." This is now trumped by the platinum standard of "Do unto others as they want done."

Another quick example will demonstrate this.

I was invited to offer my "Top of the Line Customer Service" program to food service workers at a large, well-known tourist attraction. The attraction had added the moniker of "world famous" to the beginning of their name. It was on all of their publicity. I suggested that if they were truly "world famous," then their food service should truly be "world famous" as well and reflect POM standards.

I suggested the following test. I would visit at least 20 food servers throughout the facility and make an "unusual" request and see what transpired. The request was unusual but not beyond the abilities of the food service staff. I asked each of the food servers if I could have "a hot dog on a hamburger bun." Not rocket science. I did get what I asked for at 5 of the stands. At the other 15 stands, I received a long list of reasons why I could not have what I asked for including:

1) They needed all of the hamburger buns for hamburgers.
2) The hot dog wouldn't stay in the hamburger bun.
3) The toppings would fall out.
4) I can't do that.
5) (And my personal favorite) It is not our policy to serve hot dogs on anything other than a hot dog bun.

I always get a chuckle out of the last excuse. It basically says that it is our policy to provide a product to you in the way that we want to do it, not in the way that you want it.

Think of all the restaurants that have a "no substitutions" policy. My typical response in any of these establishments is that "my policy is not to do business with people who have that type of policy."

The majority of the food servers spent more time trying to politely explain why they couldn't do what I asked for than it would have taken for them to honor my request. Few, if any, even asked why I wanted the hot dog on the hamburger bun. Most of them were more concerned with the problems created by my request (e.g. at the end of the day, they would have one less hamburger bun and one more hot dog bun) than with pleasing me, THE CUSTOMER. POM service would have dictated that I could have my hot dog almost any way that I chose.

How would your employees respond to an unusual request like the one I made? Would they spend more time explaining to me why I couldn't have what I wanted? Or would they delightfully serve up the hot dog on a hamburger bun with a smile on their face?

At most tourist attractions, the number one question asked is not "Where is the ABC ride located?" It is "Where is the bathroom?" POM service suggests that every employee know where EVERY bathroom is located, be able to explain how to get there and, if necessary, guide the person to find it.

One of the reasons that POM service does not flow smoothly is that employees rarely see the world through the eyes of the customer. When the average employee comes to work, they don't notice small things because, to them, it is just another day at the office. They quickly go to their work area and get ready for another endless stream of customers. They do not think about what the customer is feeling. Consider these examples:

1) A financial arrangements coordinator at a doctor's office or hospital does not sense the fear and apprehension that a patient is feeling when they enter the office. They just want the patient to fill out the correct forms.

2) A plumber coming into a house to unclog an overflowing toilet does not think about how his female customer feels about having a strange man who may smell from his last job enter her home. She may wonder if his shoes are clean. The plumber just wants to unclog the toilet.

3) A clerk at a cell phone store does not think that anyone would just want to "make and take calls" on their cell phone. He may look and act as if the customer lives in a cave. He will try to tell the customer about all the other features of the phone he is pushing that day. The customer may feel that he is being mocked. The clerk was wants to reach his sales goal

I know events like these occur, because all of the above have happened to me or someone I know within the last 5 years. Do any of these employees work for you? Have they been taught to see the world through the eyes of the customer? High end hotel chains encourage their Senior Management team to work at front line jobs several times a year to see and hear what customers are saying. Several chains change General Managers often to make sure that they don't become complacent and miss things right under their noses. Herb Kelleher, the former CEO of Southwest Airlines, used to serve peanuts and pretzels on Southwest flights so that he could interact with customers and understand their experience. At other companies, employees are encouraged to use the service/buy the product provided by their company, so they will know the customer experience firsthand. POM is not going away. If you don't provide it for your customers, the competition will.

THOUGHT BOMBS TO PONDER

1) What levels of customer service do you provide? Good service (meeting the needs of the customer)? Excellent service (extending beyond their expectations)?

Top of the Line Customer Service (anticipating their next needs and providing POM? How about your competition? What level of service do they provide?

2) How often do you check with your customers to make sure that they are happy with the service that you are providing them? At Enterprise Car Rentals, at the end of every rental, customers are asked if the service rated a 10 on a 1 to 10 scale. If you say no, they will want to know why. That is the mark of an organization that continuously wants to improve.

3) How well do you respond to unusual customer requests? Do your policies preclude your employees' ability to truly offer the customer what he/she wants?

4) How much training have you provided your service providers? The basics? More? Do they ever get a chance to see the world through the customer's eyes?

5) Do your customer service employees really like dealing with customers? How do you know?

CHAPTER 13

GOING THE EXTRA MILE

COMMON SENSE

Customers expect more than they ever did. Most companies pay close attention to competitive pricing, offering sales, discounts and bulk rates. They offer "frequent user" rewards to keep customers coming back. They will use loss leaders to bring new customers into the establishment in the hope that they will be able to retain them.

UNCOMMON SENSE

Price, rewards, discounts and rebates certainly matter. However, giving a customer a "WOW" experience will go a long way further. Organizations that think about amazing their customers will stand out from the crowd. Customers now shift their loyalties regularly. The major reason customers leave their old service provider is because they were not treated in a "special" way.

Exceptional people and exceptional organizations are always willing to go farther than their competition. Some do it for business purposes. Some do it because they believe it is the right thing to do and part of the credo of the organization. Some do it because it feels good. There are many reasons to "go the extra mile." The issue is not the intention of the service provider but the impact of their actions. There are many people and organizations with good intentions to do the right thing. Good intentions are great but are not meaningful unless they are coupled with outstanding impact.

Consider this example.

An associate of mine, Alan B., travels to fine hotels around the world. He works in the hotel industry and is quite sensitive to the nuances of exceptional service. He was sitting by the pool at a four-star resort on vacation with his family and chose to order a "Bloody Mary with extra black pepper" at the pool one morning. Since he was intrigued by the book he was reading, he paid minimal attention to the waiter who brought the drink. He signed the check to his room and promptly forgot about the entire interaction. No "WOWs" so far. Later that afternoon, he went back to the pool and continued reading. He did not request beverage service. There was a new waiter on duty. The WOW came when the new waiter caught his eye and quickly said, "Mr. B., let me know if I can bring you another "Bloody Mary with extra black pepper."

Alan had not mentioned his name to either waiter and yet both waiters knew his name and his drink. You might expect this type of service at your local hometown bar, but it truly was a WOW at a hotel 3,000 miles from home. Feeling like he was being treated well, Alan ordered two more Bloody Mary's with extra pepper, tipped the second waiter generously and informed the general manager of the hotel about the exceptional service he had received. Now that is Win/Win/Win for all involved. The customer, the waiter and the hotel all won. WOW service usually results in a WIN for everyone involved.

Here is another example.

An extremely popular restaurant in Kansas City was quite busy on most weekend nights. Even if you had a reservation, there was no guarantee that you would be seated at your designated time. The restaurant was a high end steak house with pleasant ambiance and extraordinary beef. The average restaurant makes much more money on what you are drinking than on what you are eating. This is especially the case for a high end restaurant with a good wine list. The owner of the restaurant, Dave, often worked at the front of the house on busy nights to make sure that customers were treated exceptionally well. The problem of late seating was always a delicate problem and had to be handled with finesse.

In many restaurants, patrons are simply asked to wait in the bar where they are likely to order and consume at least one extra drink person while they are waiting for their table. The restaurant benefits from the extra revenue, but some of the customers feel like the reservation they made was pointless. Dave was not satisfied with this idea and found a way to turn a potential problem into the Win/Win/Win solution that had a definite WOW attached to it.

If you had an 8:00PM reservation at the restaurant and Dave was not able to seat you within 5 minutes of your designated time, Dave would personally come over to you and your party and say, "I want to thank you personally for making a reservation to eat here tonight. I know that you will love your meal here. Sometimes we get so darn popular that our guests stay a bit longer than we expect. We never want anyone to rush anyone through a fine meal. We don't like to have to make our great customers wait either, so here is what I would like to do for you. With my compliments, please allow me to bring you and your party a glass of champagne to enjoy while you wait for us to get your table ready. Would that be acceptable to you?"

There's that magic word FREE again. But it was not the fact that the champagne was free that created the WOW. Free is great, but the way in Dave handled the situation made the chilled bubbly taste all the better. Other guests nearby began to hope that their table might be delayed as well. Talk about turning a problem into an opportunity. Don't think about the hit to the bottom line for all of the champagne that Dave gave away. When all was said and done, Dave's champagne sales almost doubled because one taste of good bubbly usually begets another, and those customers often ordered a bottle or two of champagne during their meal. The customers remembered Dave and the champagne and usually forgot about being seated late. Dave's demeanor mattered almost as much as the champagne because the customer felt that Dave showed empathy for their situation and sincerely wanted to do right by them.

Do your employees look for opportunities to empathize with potentially unhappy customers? Are they willing and able to provide care and concern when potential problem situations arise? Are they clever enough to find ways where all the parties come out better?

It can be something simple. A parent buys an ice cream cone for her child, and before they leave the store, the child drops it on the floor. The child feels embarrassed and now thinks that the ice cream is gone. The mother is frustrated and gets ready to scold the child about being so careless. A potential customer meltdown is happening right in front of your eyes. Would your counter person notice such an event and immediately reassure both child and parent that "people drop their cones all the time. No big deal. How about if I get you another one? I'll even throw in some sprinkles (or another new topping)." Problem avoided. Mother and child relieved. Win/Win/Win for everyone.

Perhaps the best illustration of this principle that I have seen in years comes from a local bank. Bankers are not always known for their sensitivity. However, this situation was different. A 10-year-old boy named Juan walked into the branch lobby with the intention of opening up a savings account with the $10 he had just earned raking up his neighbor's leaves. He walked in, proud of his accomplishment and eager to go home and show his mom his new bank book. When Juan got to the counter, he reached into his pocket to give the teller his $10 only to find that the $5 bill and the 5 $1 bills that were there when he left home were now gone. He burst into tears, distraught at the turn of events.

The teller, Toby, had several choices. She could have:

1) Told Juan to retrace his steps so that he might be able to find his money.
2) Given him empathy telling him how sorry she was that the money was gone.
3) Asked Juan if he had "left the money at home."
4) Simply said "Next."

None of these actions would have resulted in Win/Win/Win. But they all would have fit within reasonable protocols. Toby was not responsible for people losing their money or claiming that they had money when they didn't. Although it was a sad turn of events, it was not her personal responsibility to make Juan's situation better.

Being a mom herself, Toby thought about Juan's plight for a moment and responded from her heart instead of from the bank's protocol. She reached into her purse, pulled out $10 and used it to open up an account for him. She told him that if he found the money later, = he should come back and give it back to her. At the end of the transaction, Juan had his bank book with a $10 deposit, and Toby had done her random act of kindness. Toby gave it no more thought and continued to process transactions for the rest of the day. End of story? Not by a long shot.

Juan went home and told his mom what had happened. She was very moved by the kindness that Toby had shown her son. She returned to the bank the next day, gave Toby $10 and told her how much she appreciated her heartfelt gesture. She said her son had worked hard for the money and would have been crest fallen if he had not received his bank book. She personally went to the branch manager and told her about what Toby had done. She also wrote a letter to the Customer Service department of the bank and detailed how much she appreciated what had occurred.

Here is what happened after that:

1) Toby received an "on the spot" reward from her local branch manager.
2) Toby received another small monetary reward from the division level.
3) Toby's act received coverage in the monthly bank newsletter.
4) Toby's act received local media coverage in the newspaper and from a local television channel.

More importantly,

5) Juan had his bank book with a $10 deposit.
6) Juan's mother was likely to have a long term relationship with the bank.
7) The bank received the kind of terrific publicity that can't be bought even with a sizeable PR budget.

That is truly Win/Win/Win. When was the last time that you or employees did something like that?

THOUGHT BOMBS TO PONDER:

1) When was the last time you went out of your way to do something extraordinary for a customer of yours? What was the reaction of the customer? How did you feel?
2) Do the service protocols at your organization encourage employees to go above and beyond customer expectations?
3) What is your attitude when you extend beyond typical service levels? Are you delighted to do so or do you so begrudgingly?
4) Do you look for opportunities to provide WOW's to your customers?
5) Think of what would be a WOW for you. Would you do that for a customer?

CHAPTER 14

HOW MUCH DO YOU LIKE TO LISTEN TO YOUR CUSTOMERS?

COMMON SENSE

Good restaurants focus on providing high quality food at appropriate prices with good ambiance. Once they have a winning combination, they just need to stick with it.

UNCOMMON SENSE

Unless you are constantly checking with your customers, you won't have any way of knowing what is working and what is not working at your restaurant.

Most staff at restaurants are not trained to query customers in such a way that they can give feedback to the chef and the management team. Therefore you are left with the customer response survey forms that are only filled out by 4% of your customers, namely the 2% that were nearly poisoned and hated their meal and the 2% that thought it was the best meal they had in the last 30 days. Neither of that type of feedback is helpful because you have not heard from the critical 96% that thought the meal was just OK.

Think of your last visit to your local mall. You went into a clothing store and were immediately assaulted by a pimpled, freckle-faced teenager who had been scripted to ask, "Hi. Welcome to Clothes Are Us. How can I help you?" If they really looked like they wanted to help me, I would be thrilled. But since this same phrase has been repeated at least 50 times to prior customers that day, this teenager is now hoping that you will say, "I'm just looking." To make sure that I make their day memorable, I typically say, "Go as far away from me as you can, as quickly as you can. Thanks." In this way we both get what we want. I am not being hassled by an employee who doesn't really care about me and would tell me that I looked good if I wrapped myself in a wad of bubble wrap. The employee gets to wander off and deal with the next customer who walks into the store.

I also love going into my local fast food store. I won't say which one, just that the name rhymes with YechDonald's. You could actually go into one of these establishments and order 600 hamburgers, 200 orders of French fries and 200 drinks, and the clerk at the counter has been told to ask you, "How about an apple turnover with that?" I go nuts when this occurs and typically answer, "Sure I'll take an apple turnover. They didn't have them in prison. I just got out last week. You know what I was in there for? Killing a fast food clerk who asked me if I wanted an apple turnover." Amazingly, I am often given the apple turnover for free. I am kidding, but you get the point. When service staff are scripted and offer their trite comments with no feeling or interest, it turns off a lot of customers.

Despite all of that, I love working with waiters and waitresses in restaurants. I just wish that I had a dollar for each time I have heard the "tip diminishing line" of "Was everything OK with your meal?' There are only 2 answers to that question- both bad. The most probable answer (assuming that you have not poisoned the person's food) is "yes" or "sure, which translates into English as "please go away." The second answer is "no" and this means there is a problem which now requires your immediate attention. The major problem with either approach is that it doesn't create rapport, warm fuzzies, interest in dessert, more drinks at a later time or a larger than 15% tip.

Consider this example.

I worked with a hotel in Southern California that had a nice restaurant on the first floor. The chef went out of his way to create an extraordinary menu with unusual offerings (compared to other restaurants in the immediate geographical area) such as Wiener Schnitzel garnished with cornichons, served with dumplings, raclette and a spectacular osso buco. To top the meal off, he prepared a fresh "to die for" tiramisu pastry daily.

The problem was that the typical patrons were single, seemingly lonely businessmen passing through town working either at the local military base or as a salesman. Their typical order would be a burger (cheeseburger if they were ready to splurge), fries and a coke. Some would order beers, but the special meals prepared by the chef were rarely tasted. After bringing them their order, the waitresses would ask, "Is everything OK?" The reply would be a muffled "Yes." Few of the patrons ever even asked to see the dessert tray with the wonderful tiramisu. There were 5 other delicious offerings included on the dessert tray as well. The owner was constantly surprised and disappointed because he knew that the tiramisu was first rate.

After eating at the restaurant a few times while I was working at the hotel, I made the following recommendations:

1) Have the waitresses really engage the patrons in conversation early in the meal. They could describe how much they enjoyed eating at the restaurant and describe their favorite meals.
2) Instead of asking "Is everything OK?" ask the patrons about small nuances of the meal. This might be hard if they ordered burgers, fries and a coke but would be easy if the customer ventured into some of the more unusual offerings. Sample questions could be:
   a) Did you enjoy the cornichons with your Weiner Schnitzel?
   b) Did you like the cheese we used in the raclette?
   c) The chef was thinking about making the sauce with the dumplings a little spicier. What do you think?
   d) Did the osso buco just fall off the bone?

The exact nature of the question isn't critical. What is critical is engaging the customer in a dialog where she could solicit and value his opinion. Feedback could also be given to the chef if the patron actually had a novel opinion. This brief interaction would open the door for the introduction of the dessert tray.

3) Instead of asking the patron whether or not they wanted to see the dessert tray, the waitresses were encouraged to bring it out as a courtesy. If the customer said they were full

> or didn't want dessert, the waitresses were encouraged to say, "You were such a GREAT customer telling me what you thought about your meal that I want to do something nice for you. Let me bring you a FREE taste of our famous tiramisu. This way the next time you are in town, you will want to leave room for it when you order your meal. It would be my pleasure to bring it to you and of course it's on the house."

It should come as no surprise that once the patron tasted the tiramisu, he was much more likely to order a piece right then and there and not wait until his next trip into town. He might also order another beer or cup of coffee to enjoy with the tiramisu. The bottom line result for this strategy was an increase in tiramisu sales of 37% and an increase in after dinner beverage sales of 14%. From the waitress' perspective, tips also increased by 20% resulting in a Win/Win/Win outcome for all concerned.

THOUGHT BOMBS TO PONDER

1) Think of how you engage your customers. What phrases do you use over and over again?
2) Do these phrases generate conversation with customers? Think of how early in the interaction this engagement occurs. Most importantly does this engagement result in encouraging repeat business or "upselling" possibilities?
3) What product or service do you have that is your tiramisu? How could you get your customers to give it a try?
4) Are your sales people encouraged to provide feedback to the chef and management as to what is selling and what is not selling?
5) Is everyone focused on Win/Win/Win outcomes or just following their scripts?

CHAPTER 15

DEALING WITH DIFFICULT SITUATIONS

COMMON SENSE

When a person has a problem, the most important thing to do is to solve the problem as quickly and efficiently as you can.

UNCOMMON SENSE

Solving the problem matters, but how the person is treated while you are solving the problem matters even more.

Imagine flying all day and arriving in a city across the country. As you watch the other passengers claim their luggage from the carousel, you are getting excited about arriving at your hotel. All of a sudden, the conveyor belt stops moving, but your luggage has not appeared. This is a less than happy moment for you as you slowly trudge to the baggage claim office. Your mood is less than optimal, and, to your dismay, you find that you are the 4th person on line to file a report. The prospect of having no toiletries and wearing the same clothes to work tomorrow is less than appealing. Although tracking and recovering your luggage is the priority, you would prefer to be served by an agent that at least gives the illusion of caring. Unless they have been trained properly, the agent there is as unhappy as you are, realizing the sudden unexpected increase in their workload. Any frustration on your part is likely to be met with the attitude of "Hey, don't be angry with me. I didn't lose your luggage." The prospect of dealing with 5 angry and frustrated customers is not very appealing to this employee.

When I worked with a highly regarded airline on the West Coast, I was invited to participate in the development of a training program that was intended to help these agents process these claims in less than 4 minutes. The UnCommon Sense aspect of the program is that it trained employees to be concerned with calming the customers down BEFORE dealing with the lost luggage. Showing care and concern for the customer's plight was essential. Customers want to feel that their frustration is understood.

The acronym for the model is LENSA, and it can be used to deal with 80% of unhappy customers in almost any venue. Why only 80%? 10% of customers have a benefit/payoff for staying angry, and there is little that can be done to appease those customers in the midst of the problem. They think they have leverage by using their anger. At times, letters of apology and future product discounts may offset some of their anger, but these people feel there is a benefit to hanging on to their anger. Another 10% of service problems have great complexity and are not going to be resolved on the spot. No simple model will address all of the idiosyncrasies associated with complex problems. However, calming down the other 80% would be terrific, if it could be accomplished on the spot in a relatively straightforward manner.

Here are some of the assumptions of the model:

1) The emotional issues must be addressed BEFORE the logical issues are addressed, or the customer will not feel good after the interaction, even if the problem is solved. When service providers are perceived as uncaring, customers are significantly less likely to "forgive" service errors. Nowhere is this clearer than when looking at medical malpractice suits. Doctors who are perceived as arrogant and non-caring are more likely to be sued for malpractice than kind and compassionate doctors who committed the same error. We are willing to forgive a caregiver whom we like or whom we feel cares about us more than a caregiver who does not seem to care about us.

2) If the person is angry, it is better to let them get as angry as they are going to get by listening and asking questions, as opposed to trying to calm them down quickly. Although service providers do not like dealing with angry customers, some customers feel the need to vent how they feel before

they are ready to work on finding a solution. We have certainly seen this in the political posturing currently taking place in Washington DC and other state capitals. Trying to offer empathy or solutions before the person is ready to hear them is the equivalent of turning on your transmitter when there are no receivers around.

3) Empathy sentences have a short half-life. Basically they can only be used twice in any conversation before they become trite and useless. I will identify the 2 ½ sentences of empathy that have the greatest impact shortly, but don't be tempted to use them too early. If the person has not fully vented their anger and you start to say "I can understand how you feel," you will be greeted with strong language indicating that they have not yet finished telling you how they feel. The perfect time to use the empathy sentences is right after the person has purged all of their anger. Saying the empathy sentences at that time can calm the person down quickly.

4) Reading body language is the key throughout the process. Although the model specifies one critical juncture when reading body language is most vital, it is really your best clue as to how the customer is feeling throughout the process and will help you recognize when the customer is most likely to be willing to work with you to solve their problem.

5) It is significantly better to focus your conversation on what you CAN do, before you tell the customer what you CAN'T do. Too many service providers believe that citing the policy of "what they can't do" will get them "off the hook." When a person says that policy does not allow them to do what you are asking, I always respond with the notion that I don't do business with companies that have policies like that. My favorite example of this is when a waiter tells me that there are no substitutions on menu items. I remind them that I am often asking for a "cheaper" option (i.e., pasta instead of steamed vegetables). I remind them that their policy is costing their organization cold hard cash, not to mention the cost of lost good will.

6) It is important for service providers to realize that they are the shock absorbers for their organizations. They are on the front

line accepting the responsibility for others who may have made errors. It is critical to be able to provide empathy and understanding to customers without taking it too personally. Employees who feel that they are constantly taking a beating at work come home and do not provide optimal caring and support to their loved ones. The state DMV and federal IRS employees may be the stellar examples here.

7) At times these heated interactions become more adversarial than cooperative. The service provider who takes the customer's frustrated comments personally wants to teach the customer a lesson. The service provider begins to see the customer as part of the problem. Great service can only be offered when the service provider joins with the customer to attack the problem together in a cooperative way. Think of a situation when the customer thinks they are right and claims that the service provider is wrong. While the service provider knows the truth, they often behave in a way which causes the customer to lose face. The net result is that the actual problem was solved, but the customer did not feel good about it. Bad will is incurred, and everyone loses in that type of interaction.

8) The mark of a great service provider is to be able to give great service to a jerk who doesn't deserve it. Let's be clear that the real reason for a provider to give great service is so they can have a great day and go home happy. Clearly it helps the company in terms of customer retention, but the key point is staff retention and satisfaction. Staff who are regularly unsettled and unhappy with their jobs because of the "abuse" that they absorb quickly move on. Well-trained staff delight at the prospect of working with difficult customers and situations and exercising their service skills. Enough assumptions already. Here is the LENSA model:

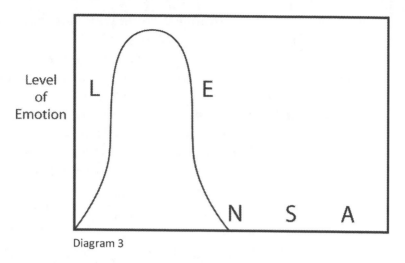

Diagram 3

The model describes how the unhappy customer moves from getting angry to getting their problem resolved. The 5 phases to the model are:

L stands for listen and ask questions.

The first phase deals with the customer from the time they arrive to the time that they reach their peak anger/frustration point. Service providers may not enjoy dealing with an angry person who tells them "not to be angry" or "that they have no right to be angry at them." Such tactics only inflame the anger and cause it to burn more brightly.

Consequently, there are only three tactics that should be used during the first phase. They are:

1) Listening carefully for the problem description (from the customer's point of view) and for the feelings engendered by the problem. The more accurate the service provider is in understanding the problem and how the person feels about it, the less anger they will have to deal with. During this phase, the active listening skill of RESTATING is valuable. Restating the problem in a simple manner demonstrates that

you have heard the customer and that you understand his/her concerns.

2) Asking questions about the problem shows that you are truly trying to understand the customer's concerns. It shows care and curiosity and that you are sincere in your attempts to handle the issue. Keep the questions open ended so that they encourage the customer to keep talking. Asking forced choice questions or trying "prove a point" to the customer is not helpful here. It is not a debate, and no prizes will be awarded for showing the customer that they are wrong.

3) In some cases, it is a good idea to "pour oil on the fire" to get the anger out faster. Simply asking "Is there anything else you are angry about?" will likely get the customer to their peak anger moment quicker. As long as the customer is not likely to harm the service provider physically, accelerating the anger causes it to burn out faster. Don't use this tactic unless you are comfortable dealing with anger issues.

E stands for empathy.

The second phase begins as soon as the customer has reached the peak of their anger. Once you are sure that you understand the problem and how the customer feels about it, three empathic sentences can be used to get the customer ready to move quickly on to solving the problem:

1) *"I can understand how _____(insert the feeling word that they have used such as frustrated, angry, cheated, betrayed, lied to etc.) when _____ (summarize what they believe the problem is here)."*

The purpose of this sentence is to demonstrate that you have accurately understood the situation and their emotional response to it. Do not patronize the customer or minimize the problem here. This will only frustrate the customer and cause them to want to vent more anger at you.

2) *"I would feel the same way as you do if I were in your situation."*

> The purpose of this sentence is to join them in their feelings. Customers are far less likely to vent anger at people who are like them and agree with them. They are far more likely to calm down at this point. However, don't say this sentence if you would not feel the way they do. The model is not about lying or placating. It is about sincere, heartfelt responses.

3) *"I can help you _____ (insert a magic word like faster, easier, more completely) if you _____ (give them an action to do to see if they are ready to move on to solve the problem).*

> In the airline example, asking them to complete the lost luggage form that begins the tracking process is the necessary first step. In a department store, the first step may be presenting the receipt for damaged/unsatisfactory goods. What you really might like to say is "If you are done yelling at me, we can start to solve your problem." However, saying it that directly will be less likely to generate the cooperation that you need from the customer.

It is important to understand that these three sentences, which can be effectively delivered within 20-30 seconds, can only be used twice in any conversation before they lose their potency. Once you have said them twice, your credibility has been dramatically reduced. The mistake made here is that some service providers try to use these sentences while the person is still upset during the "L" phase. If they have not finished telling you their side of the story and you claim to understand, you will be greeted by "You don't understand anything."

N is for read the nonverbal signals.

The best indicator that the person is ready to solve the problem is that their body language visibly changes once they have calmed down. Some examples of positive body language changes are:

1) Speaking more softly
2) Speaking more slowly
3) Pausing between sentences
4) Using less volatile language and tone
5) Uncrossing their arms
6) Making direct eye contact and looking at you, instead of looking away
7) Being less flushed in the face
8) Showing less tension in their jaws and other facial muscles
9) Interrupting less often
10) Using smaller gestures
11) Not resorting to repeated random energy gestures (i.e. Finger tapping, hand wringing, foot tapping, hand washing, ring playing.)
12) Being less angry in their facial expressions.

There are probably many more body language cues that you could look for. Any good book on reading body language will provide an entire catalogue of other behaviors to look for. Don't react to the first sign of relaxation. Wait until you see at least 3 separate body language cues before moving on to the next step.

Another important issue is that if you have been watching their body language straight through the interaction, it will much easier for you at this point. You will able to see small gradual changes as opposed to looking for major changes. You will also know which behaviors are most connected with their anger by watching how they behave during the "L" phase. This is why it is usually easier to solve problems in person than on the phone or by email. Most unhappy customers will find it much easier to make nasty comments on the phone or through an email when they don't have to say it directly to you. If you have a choice, offer to meet with the unhappy customer in person.

Hopefully, you have been modeling the body language you wish to receive in return. Sometimes your negative body language can prolong the emotional part of the problem. A good exercise is to videotape your body language during a customer interaction and then view it to see if your body language is appropriate and neutral.

Using a mirror to check your "phone smile" can also be helpful if you work on the phone. When you are working behind a counter, desk or computer, it may be hard for the customer to see your body language. It may be hard for you to see their body language. If this is the case, extra care should be placed on voice cues given and received. If possible, move out from behind the obstacle at times as well.

If you still perceive negative body language, return to do more of the "L" and "E" phases. Perhaps they have not yet purged all of their feelings. Also remember that 10% of the population will choose to remain angry thinking that it gives them leverage during the problem solving phase. If you think you are dealing with this type of person, move into the next phase or pass the customer on to a supervisor.

S stands for seeking solutions.

Hopefully, by the time you have reached this phase, you are dealing with a calmer customer who is now focused on problem resolution. Here are a few guidelines to help you through this phase:

1) If possible offer at least three options, not just one. Those options should include Best Case Scenario, Worst Case Scenario and Most Probable Case Scenario. It is important to present these options in that order to demonstrate that you have a variety of approaches that are possible. Be honest, and let the customer know what is involved with each option.

2) Always let the customer know what you can and are willing to do before you tell them what you can't do. If you start off by reminding them of what you can't do, their mood may shift, and they may begin to doubt whether or not you really want to help them. There is a time to set boundaries and limits to the help that you can provide, but that time is not at the beginning of this phase. Some customers believe that they are entitled to free or discounted service as soon as an error has occurred. Some believe that the louder they complain or the more they ask to see your supervisor, the more likely they

will be to get something for free. Care should be exercised here. Mistakes do occur. However, not every error warrants a free or discounted service.

3) If possible, let the customer choose the option they prefer. In a situation where the customer feels out of control, giving them the choice of next steps begins to restore their faith.

4) Apologies may be in order here. However, it is hard for a service provider to apologize when they do not feel that they were responsible for the error. Sometimes an apology in the name of the organization is easier to offer.

5) Letting the customer know that you will make Senior Management aware of the problem often helps as well. In this manner, the customer may feel vindicated that because they spoke up, others will not have to endure the same inconvenience. Telling them to write a letter may show them that you don't have a personal stake in remediating the situation.

A stands for action.

In this phase, you must tell the customer what you are going to do. Until this point, everything else has just been talk. Action always speaks louder than words. Show them that you will stay on top of the problem until it is solved. Ask them how they would like to kept informed as the problem resolution proceeds. Would they prefer a phone call or text from you when you have more information? When you commit to solve a problem by a certain time and are unable to do so, communicate with them and let them know what has happened. While they may be disappointed that you were not able to fully resolve the issue within the stated time frame, they will at least feel that you have not forgotten or forsaken them and are still on top of the issue.

The attitude you display while taking action matters as much as the action itself. Service providers who delight in handling problems are viewed significantly differently than providers who take action begrudgingly. Suggesting that "it would be my pleasure to help you" goes a long way towards converting what was a problem into a memorable experience for the customer. It validates the customer's belief that the issue was significant and that it deserved care and attention. Concluding the action by asking the customer if there is anything else that needs to happen leaves the customer feeling like they are important.

THOUGHT BOMBS TO PONDER

1) If you are service provider, think of how you react during difficult situations. Would you like to be helped by a person like you? How about your organization? Does it react in a caring and compassionate manner, or does it seem to be annoyed at having to deal with the issue?. The customer's perception of you and your organization are at stake every time there is a problem. The best organizations look for opportunities to turn complainers into good will ambassadors.

2) How comfortable are you when dealing with an angry customer or a difficult situation? Do you feel comfortable that you can calm them down?

3) Do you take customer comments personally? Do you resent having to accept responsibility for problems that you did not create? When you go home, does your work leave you feeling angry and unable to provide caring and support for the people at home?

4) How skilled are you at reading body language? Are you intuitive enough to know when a person has calmed down?

5) Do you enjoy solving problems? Do you enjoy flexing your service provider skills during the most difficult interactions?

CHAPTER 16

TRANSFORMING THE CULTURE OF YOUR ORGANIZATION

COMMON SENSE

Strong leaders who have clear optimistic vision and positive action plans can come into an organization and gradually change the culture.

UNCOMMON SENSE

Clear vision is great, but the fastest way to transform your organization is to first listen and then "pulse" the organization so that you understand current concerns. After you have shown humility by being a sincere student of the organization first, the organization may be more likely to embrace you as a teacher afterwards.

An airline had been run by an autocratic CEO, Howard, for many years. He was a former military man and strongly believed in the credos of chain of command and need to know. He had surrounded himself with vice presidents who were his sole contact with rank and file employees. There are many dangers in this style of leadership. Information coming upstream and downstream was filtered by each of the vice presidents, resulting in communication disconnects and dead ends. Howard was shielded from many problems and issues because he was known to have a bad temper and was usually more interested in finding the person responsible and affixing blame than on growing people through conflict to find a solution. Problems can be opportunities to grow future leaders, if handled correctly.

This example deals with how to transform a leadership culture. The autocratic CEO retired after a long and distinguished career, and a new leader, Rusty, was selected. Rusty was well known in the industry but was an outsider to this organization. His initial selection was greeted with skepticism. Many Senior Level Leaders were concerned about how much change he was going to implement.

However, his initial behavior began to create a healthy, welcomed culture change in the entire organization by using UnCommon Sense. It didn't happen overnight, but it did happen faster than anyone had imagined.

Most new executives would begin their first day at work by arriving at 8:00 or 9:00 AM and immediately meeting with Senior Leaders to begin to understand and assess current issues. That would be Common Sense. Rusty had an entirely different view as to how to gather information AND quickly sent a message to the entire organization. At 4:00 AM on his first day, he took off his jacket and tie, rolled up his shirt sleeves and quietly walked into the airport (located near company headquarters) and began to seek out 3rd shift maintenance staff. In the entire time that Howard had been in charge, he had never bothered to come and visit 3rd shift personnel and certainly never engaged line employees in conversation. Howard wanted and expected everyone to follow chain of command and pass appropriate information up the chain through their supervisors and managers. Howard accepted the data he received without ever reality testing it.

Rusty had a significantly different style. He walked up to as many employees as he could find and introduced himself as the new CEO for the airline. He then stuck out his hand, asked them their names and greeted each person warmly. He told them how much he appreciated their dedication and hard work. He then asked each of them to tell him what he needed to know in order to make the best decisions possible for the airline.

The employees were shocked. No one from Senior Leadership had ever visited them. Certainly no one had ever asked for their input. They had simply gone about their work. Rusty also presented each of the employees with his business card and suggested that they give him a call if they wanted to provide further information that they deemed important.

Although the impact on 3rd shift employees was tremendous, the impact on everyone else was even stronger. At 8:00 AM when Senior Leaders began to arrive at work, word of the new CEO's visit to 3rd shift had already spread throughout the company. Senior Leaders began asking, "He went to visit 3rd shift. Who did he speak to? What did they say? What was he looking for?" The idea that he wanted to gather input from all levels directly instead of using chain of command was an unsettling surprise to the Senior Leaders.

At his first meeting, he was asked to explain (and defend) his actions. Rusty responded with a smile saying that, although he trusted his Senior Leaders, he wanted input from every level of the organization and wanted to make sure that he understood what everyone felt. In this way, he could bring everyone together, encourage buy in and help guide the organization in new, more open directions. Additionally, he asked each member of his team to get out of their offices, put "boots on the ground" and get the pulse of what was happening inside their areas. Rusty wanted to make sure that he heard from at least 80% of the employees, either on his own or through the walk and talk sessions. Although there was wariness, great suspicion and skepticism at first, the Senior Leaders complied. Although it took a while for the spirit of open communication to become part of the culture, in the long run, the organization was able to make quicker and more widely accepted decisions. Rusty continued to get out of his office to chat with employees in many different departments, both in the corporate headquarters and around their entire system.

In the beginning, much of what was communicated had to do with unheard complaints and long standing dissatisfactions. This was to be expected, due to the policies and protocols of the previous CEO. Those issues needed to be vented. Hearing those concerns made it clear to Rusty that employees had not felt appreciated and valued. That became his first order of business. It is hard to get employees to buy in to new innovative, service oriented concepts unless they felt like they are a valuable part of the team. While some members of the Senior Leaders did not appreciate what they considered "whining" from their departments, airing of old concerns quickly transitioned into moving forward.

This strategy is NOT about being nice or winning popularity contests. It is about regaining trust and building confidence so that problems can be identified and dealt with in a more positive manner. This strategy was originally described 30 years ago in the classic book "In Search Of Excellence" by Tom Peters and Robert Waterman as Management by Walking Around (MBWA.)

I will offer the UnCommon Sense version of MBWA and re-title it LBWA (Leadership by Walking Around). I usually suggest to all leadership personnel that they spend a minimum of 1-3 hours weekly engaging in LBWA activities. I usually go further and suggest that any leader found in their own office for the majority of each work day ought to be relieved of their leadership responsibilities. Management and/or leadership rarely occurs when you stay in your own office. Clearly, there are days when meetings and reports demand your full attention, but the message should be that leaders need to be out and about chatting, training, cheerleading and participating in LBWA activities.

When a leader goes out to visit an employee, there are typically 4 different types of meetings that are held. They are:

1) Social calls
2) Status checks
3) Constructive Feedback and/or "Butt chewing"
4) LBWA visits

I encourage leaders to let their employees know exactly what type of meeting it is going to be prior to the visit so that the employee can prepare appropriately. It is also important not to conduct more than one type of business at each meeting. For instance, if a leader starts a meeting as a social visit, the employee may spend most of this time wondering what the "real purpose" of the meeting is and miss the opportunity to enjoy the social call.

Here is a brief description of the 4 types of meetings:

SOCIAL CALLS

Social calls help you to learn about your employees. They are critical to starting or continuing personal relationships. Employees who feel that their leaders care about them are more likely to be responsive to informational or work requests. One of the most valuable benefits to having strong personal relationships is that employees who feel that they are trusted are often more willing to identify problems. Social calls involve talking about family, hobbies, interests, sports teams and other areas of mutual interest. When you let an employee know that your visit is strictly a social call, they can relax without waiting for the "other shoe" to drop. They know that business will not be discussed.

STATUS CHECKS

Status checks involve catching up on the progress of a work-related activity. The leader may want to know the status of a project in terms of timeline, resources used, specs, budget considerations or other work details. When an employee understands that this is the nature of the meeting, they can be expected to gather all relevant data to make the meeting effective and efficient. There is little need for social conversation or chit chat. The participants can get down to business quickly and terminate the meeting once the status is reviewed and action items are assigned (if necessary.)

BUTT CHEWING

Constructive feedback and/or "Butt chewing" meetings are held when the leader is concerned/unhappy about something. These meetings should be handled in a caring manner. The impact of the meeting is to understand the problematic issue at hand and come to an agreement as to how it will be handled. While some consultants encourage the "sandwich technique" of starting and ending the meeting on a lighter note to lessen the blow, I have found that when most employees know that something is wrong, they would rather deal with it directly. Opening a meeting with small talk when there is a major disconnect often leads to unnecessary anxiety for the employee while they wait to find out the real cause of the discontent. If there is a problem, it should be addressed directly.

LBWA

LBWA is the type of meeting that is focused on one question: "What obstacles are getting in your way?" The purpose of this meeting is to identify problems early so that there is a maximum amount of time and options available to solve the problem. When employees and leaders have had social meetings and are in a trusted relationship, LBWA is an invaluable tool. If a leader does not have a relationship with employees that has served to establish and build trust, the leader will not find out about problems until after they occur or when they can no longer be hidden. Without trust, employees are concerned about blame and wonder what will happen to them if they identify a problem.

In "blamecentric" organizations, problems are not identified early. Consider the difference between that kind of organization and one where early problem identification is welcomed, appreciated and valued. In the manufacturing plant of a name brand electronics manufacturer, any employee working on an assembly line is encouraged to "stop the line" if they see a defect. Despite the fact that "stopping the line" for more than 15 minutes can quickly result in a six figure deduction, almost straight from the bottom line, employees are encouraged to do so. It is considered far better to catch a defect while the product is still on the line than after it has been delivered to customers. The company adopted the slogan of "hug the defect identifier" as a way of honoring employees who take responsibility and step up.

When you do an LBWA visit, I encourage you to ask the critical question and then write down the response, assuming that you get a response. The first time you do a LBWA visit, the employee may be skeptical or not understand what you are asking or why you are asking it. In fear-based organizations, employees will likely say that everything is fine and then ask their colleagues why they think you are snooping around. What have they heard? If this is the response you get, thank the employee and tell them you will return again with the same question at another time. If the employee thinks of issues to share, tell them that you would be delighted to listen at that time. Employees should NOT be coerced into talking about obstacles. When they trust you and are ready to share their ideas, they will talk.

The first time they are willing to share ideas, the concerns may be very general or long standing complaints. This is testing behavior to see how you will react. It is important to write down their concerns even if they are general and there is nothing that you can do about them. This shows that you are serious about the process. You might also offer empathy and say, "I can see how these issues might be upsetting or troublesome, but I am not sure that I can do anything about resolving them." It is important to be straightforward and honest at this point. Don't tell them that you will look into issues, unless you really intend to. Suggest to them that you would be quite willing to address issues more within your sphere of influence. Ask them to think about those issues for your next visit. Don't mock them for raising issues that you can't change. You want to show your seriousness and commitment to helping them during each visit, which in the long run, will be appreciated.

At some point, they will share real concerns. Thank them for doing so and identify the easiest one to solve. If you know what you will do, let them know the action you will take. Tell them you will report on progress as it occurs. Identify other issues that you will tackle and give them your action plan, if you already know what you will do. If you need to consider several options, tell them that you will keep them apprised of the situation. Identify issues that will require the involvement of others. Tell them which issues you may not be able to handle. All of these responses will help you build trust and credibility with your employees.

When you return for your next round of visits (hopefully within the next week or so), tell them the progress you have made. When they see that you have listened to them and responded with actions, they will be more likely to identify other issues early. LBWA begins to yield bottom line savings by the 3rd or 4th visit. After that, it continues to be one of the best ROIT (Return On Invested Time) strategies in your tool box. Think carefully about which employees will provide the best information to you about obstacles. Schedule to see them regularly.

THOUGHT BOMBS TO PONDER:

1) How often do Senior Leaders in your organization go out and "pulse" their employees? How open are they to hearing concerns and complaints? When was the last time your CEO was out shaking hands with your 3rd shift employees?
2) When employees talk about long standing, nagging problems, how open are you to hearing them and then raising those issues in an appropriate forum?
3) How much time do you spend in your office versus being out and about putting your "boots on the ground?"
4) When you have meetings with your employees, do you tell them the purpose of the meeting first? Do you have meetings where parts of the meetings involve more than one agenda (social calls, status, butt chewing and LBWA)?
5) Which employees would you give you the largest ROIT for your LBWA visits? How much time can you allot to LBWA visits? Do you know what to say during an LBWA visit?

CHAPTER 17

NOTHING MATTERS MORE THAN TRUST

COMMON SENSE

Most people are inherently distrustful. After all, everyone has an angle, right? It just takes a certain amount of time before you figure out what their game is. This is even more likely in the workplace than it is in personal relationships because a lot is at stake. Additionally, if you have been burned in the past, you are less likely to trust again.

UNCOMMON SENSE

Trust underlies everything in the business world. It is the unspoken foundation that all leadership activities are based on. Trust can be developed more quickly if you are conscientious about what you are doing. Trust can be earned through tangible short-term behaviors on your part in addition to consistent, long-term behaviors.

Leaders have the ability to build trusting relationships quickly with colleagues, staff and customers. This activity should be a top priority during the first 90 days of your tenure as a leader. One of the first steps to accomplish this goal includes holding "Expectations and Boundaries" meetings with your first reports and other key individuals. In such a meeting, a dialog about each of these two issues is initiated.

EXPECTATIONS

Common Sense dictates that you should discuss task expectations associated with roles and responsibilities. Leadership By Walking Around (LBWA) time and a variety of other "pulse taking" relationship activities would also be identified. Additionally, other critical issues are discussed such as:

1) Scope of job
2) Training required
3) Help needed (in terms of resources, headcount or other areas)
4) Degrees of freedom to work independently
5) Unique issues associated with the position

The UnCommon Sense "Expectations" portion of the meeting is concerned with relationship issues and involves discussion involving communication, feedback, interactions, and evaluation.

Communication

1) How often is communication desired?
2) About what topics and issues?
3) How often?
4) What level of detail?
5) What format?

Feedback

1) What type of feedback will be given?
2) How often?
3) What format will be used?
4) Any special needs and concerns when constructive or critical feedback is required?
5) From whom will feedback be collected?

Interactions

1) Meeting protocols
2) Brainstorming
3) Coaching and mentoring
4) Delegation of work
5) Negotiation and conflict resolution strategies
6) Political issues

Evaluation

After the initial meeting, it is useful to have this type of meeting again at least semi-annually (as part of the performance appraisal process). These discussions may need to be held more often, especially if there are visible disconnects between parties.

BOUNDARIES

The UnCommon Sense "BOUNDARIES" part of the meeting specifies limits in many areas such as:

1) Budget issues including discretionary spending
2) Degree of authority
3) Span of control
4) Resources available/unavailable
5) Political issues

It is usually better to specify areas of concerns BEFORE they arise. Whatever may become an issue later should be dealt with proactively, instead of reactively. Remember that it is much easier to "Lighten Controls" than it is to "Tighten Controls." Unique concerns should also be brought up here. Two of my favorites include:

1) No Surprise Policy
   Everyone makes mistakes. You should have no problems accepting that. Leaders are not "blamecentric." They do not to look for victims to blame but instead use mistakes as opportunities to grow staff. However, surprises are a different story. A surprise occurs when an employee does not tell you directly about an error that has been made or discovered. When you find out about the error from someone else or through your own devices, you may assume that the employee was "hiding" the issue. (Of course, there are certain errors that the employee may not be aware of. In that case, it would not be considered a surprise.) Consistent with the LBWA philosophy, you need to know about errors

as early as possible so that you have the maximum time, opportunity and options to help others correct them.

2) Disloyalty Policy
    You are not a perfect leader. You will make mistakes and at times make less-than-popular decisions. Hopefully, you will have no problem when any employee comes to see you and tells you privately (in a professional manner) what they think about what you have done. (As a leader, I am even OK if the employee queries which orifice in my body my head was in when I made a particular decision.) Hopefully, you can handle most comments, opinions or questions.

    If that opinion is aired outside your office, it becomes quite another matter. Now you have 2 additional problems. One problem is that, since you don't know that such an opinion has been vocalized, you can't work on doing anything about it, if you don't agree with it. The second problem is that you will have to spend extra time managing the perception of the issue. These are unnecessary uses of your time. This also creates the sense of disloyalty that begins to disconnect trust.

Following this discussion, it is a great idea to begin an open dialog about trust. Think about it. How many jobs have you had? How often was there a formal discussion about trust held at the beginning of your tenure? For most people, the answer is never or maybe once. I am continually amazed that such an important issue is left to assumption or tacit understanding. Why not put it on the table and begin to actively work on it right from the start?

Typically, trust conversations include a discussion of:

1) what we expect from each other to build and maintain trust
2) the factors that would reduce trust
3) the current trust level in the group
4) factors that have contributed to this trust level

5) activities that we can include that will build trust in the entire group
6) disconnects that exist and how we can work on re-connecting

Trust is, without question, the single most important catalyst to increase productivity and speed in the workplace. While many leaders would acknowledge this notion, activities associated with developing trust rarely show up on To Do Lists.

It is likely that most of us recognize that we have to build trust, but we are:

1) Unsure how to go about it
2) Afraid to talk about it (because that might indicate that we thought trust was low)
3) Unwilling to solicit feedback about trust levels from others
4) Certain that trust occurs naturally and we don't have much control over it.

Most people believe that trust is built only over the long haul or that it is gained as a result and by product of successful completion of work. While this can be true, trust can be developed intentionally in significantly less time rather than accidentally or incidentally.

When you have high trust, others have no need to second guess what your "real intention" is. They simply accept what is said and move on from there. There is no need to validate what has been said with three other people because trust has been earned. Trust and credibility go hand in hand.

Let's make it simple. Trust and credibility are intimately related to the following 10 factors. They are linked to your ability to demonstrate:

1) Competence
   You are:
   a) Highly skilled in your craft
   b) Viewed as an expert in your field.
2) Honesty and integrity

You are:
a) Viewed as morally principled
b) Perceived as having integrity beyond question.

3) Reliability and Consistency

You:
a) Say what you will do and then do what you said.
b) Have a proven, consistent, track record.

4) Congruence

You demonstrate:
a) Shared key values, attitudes, hopes and beliefs with others.

5) Openness

You are willing to:
a) Ask and answer the tough questions
b) Share information beyond surface issues
c) Share your "real" feelings about significant issues in a constructive manner and
d) Share privileged information with discretion when appropriate.

6) Acceptance with little or no qualification

You are:
a) Accepting of others for who they are and accepted by other for who you are.

7) Likeability

You are:
a) Enjoyable to be with
b) Pleasant, easy going, on an even emotional keel and rarely speak out or yell without thinking
c) Perceived as a "regular" person with little to no "airs" about you.

8) Objectivity/Flexibility

You:
a) React to data as a "reasonable person" would.
b) Aren't self-centered
c) Make decisions for the benefit of the group and others
d) Willing to change your mind when presented with more/ new data.

9) Enthusiasm

You:

a) Appear to be cautiously optimistic

b) Have a clear idea of where you are going and what to do next.

10) Self-sacrifice

You are:

a) Willing to sacrifice on behalf of others.

Imagine a rating scale for these ten factors from 1 through 10, with 1 being the lowest rating and 10 being the highest rating. Would your score be over 80? If so, you probably have high trust and credibility with the majority of people whom you work with and for. Although desirable, it is hard to have high credibility with everyone you work with. Whenever we disappoint someone or fail to deliver (regardless of circumstances), we often lose credibility points. Few people have a credibility score over 95.

So how do you know if you have high trust and credibility with your colleagues? Most people don't ask and assume that if there is no overt bad feedback, that their credibility is high and intact.

The following factors, however, may be indicators that your credibility has been damaged:

1) People stop asking you for your input

2) You are no longer asked to participate in certain meetings

3) When you are asked for your opinion, several others are also queried to validate your opinion

4) You are reassigned to work in the your company's Gulag (where you can cause only minimal damage)

5) When you speak at meetings, others pay less attention, roll their eyes or begin checking their "crackberries"

6) You find things out through memos and official communication because you are considered "out of the loop"

7) When you walk into certain meeting areas, the conversation suddenly changes or people begin speaking softer

8) Another person has been placed between you and your boss

9) People start avoiding you in common areas such as the lunch room, coffee spot

10) When you walk into other people's offices, other people have "less time" for you than they did previously.

If credibility has been lost by either party, there are a few more steps that need to be taken:

Credibility is very precious and can only be fully restored TWICE. The second time is much harder, and the credibility rarely returns to 100%. Therefore, great care should be exercised to keep credibility high. Consider the following 7-step model for restoring damaged credibility.

In this model, each person:

1) owns his/her own behavior
2) offers a "good faith gesture"
3) offers a plan for less hurtful/disrespectful behavior
4) changes behavior accordingly
5) works to enact new behavior for a month
6) asks the other for feedback on how the new behavior is being received and perceived and
7) agrees to participate in another meeting at some point in the future where little "itches," relapses, and/or new issues can be addressed.

OWN YOUR BEHAVIOR

It is necessary to take sincere responsibility for past behavior on an intent and impact level. Many people believe that if their intent was good, then their impact should be interpreted benevolently.

When we judge ourselves, we judge ourselves by our intentions. When we judge others, we judge them by their impact. IMPACT is the more important part.

If the other person feels hurt, then don't suggest that your intent was not meant to be hurtful. It won't be perceived that way. Sometimes an apology is in order. If you have made an error (of commission or omission), an apology to the other person may be valued. It will be taken as a sign of sincerity.

This is not about play acting, pretending, manipulating or lying. If the apology is not perceived to be sincere and heartfelt, it is better not to offer one at all.

OFFER A GOOD FAITH GESTURE

This is like a peace offering. It involves sacrificing time or effort in service of your counterpart. If I have been late in getting data to you, the next time, I can offer to submit it earlier to give you more time to deal with it. If I have not communicated about a certain topic, I can offer to meet more often or find another way to relay the information better.

The key element is that I am offering to do something for your benefit as a sign of "atonement" for past behaviors. Consider that the word "atone" can be broken up into the two words: "at one." That is what this step is designed to do: to bring you back "at one" with your counterpart.

YOUR NEW PLAN

Describe what you will DO differently to make sure that the same results do not occur again. In what way are you willing to adjust your behavior? What will you do more of? What will you do less of? How will you judge the success of your new plan?

Some people benefit from writing the plan down. Include all/any details that you are concerned about. Developing some criteria to make sure that the plan is working will help you to be more successful.

DO IT CONSISTENTLY

New behaviors take 21-30 days to take hold. Habits are not easy to break. Think about your New Year's Resolutions. Most of us stopped doing what we resolved before January 21.

Repetition makes the new behavior more likely to endure. Try to reward and encourage each other when you witness the new behavior. Be aware of obstacles that get in the way. Avoid the temptation to relapse into old behaviors. Ask for help from others if it will help to keep you on track.

ASK FOR FEEDBACK

Each person needs the opportunity to give and receive feedback about their new behaviors. Don't be ashamed or uncomfortable to ask each other, "How am I doing?" Ask about specific parts of the new behavior if you are uncertain about how/if they are being perceived.

The very fact that dialog about the issue continues is likely to be helpful. Too often people move from "I am OK with this. I don't want to deal with it. No big thing" to "Now I need to kill you" with nothing in between. The feedback process allows other potential problems/miscommunications/misperceptions (small itches) to be dealt with before they are exaggerated and blown out of proportion.

NEXT MEETING

Hopefully after feedback has been exchanged and 30 days have passed, the issue can be revisited and looked at more objectively. Perhaps other expected/unexpected issues have arisen. Perhaps intentions are being doubted. Perhaps other feelings have been generated. This is a good time to check those issues out and keep the conversation open.

Remember that credibility can only be rebuilt TWICE. It is precious and needs constant monitoring to ensure high speed and productivity in the workplace.

THOUGHT BOMBS TO PONDER

1) What is the current level of trust in your group? Between you and your first reports? Between other group members?
2) What evidence do you have to support your beliefs? Have you asked for feedback? Is this ever discussed at meetings?
3) How do you rate on the trust and credibility factors suggested? What can you do to improve your credibility?
4) Is there anyone that you work with where there is a credibility disconnect? Is it worth your time/effort to rebuild credibility?
5) How can you build trust within your group?

CHAPTER 18

TRUST BUILDING BEHAVIORS

COMMON SENSE

Trust is built over long periods of time when people clearly demonstrate consistent, objective and selfless behavior. Trust is based on watching the behavior of others, particularly when individuals make decisions to benefit others or the group as opposed to benefitting themselves.

UNCOMMON SENSE

Trust can be built intentionally. By creating and seizing opportunities to behave in a trusting manner, new managers can develop trust within their group within a short period of time.

Nothing impacts a group's ability to move quickly more than trust. It is the catalyst that accelerates action. It can serve as the lubricant for empowerment, delegation, innovation and agility. While many leaders acknowledge the need for trust, action items to build trust are rarely found on "To Do" lists. Suppose I were to ask you for a 30 day plan outlining what you expected to do to begin building more trusting relationships. Would you know where to start? Here is some help.

Here are more than 15 tangible activities that can result in increased trust if the activities are done in an honest, open and non-patronizing manner.

1) SHOW CARE, CONCERN AND COMPASSION

One of the best things a leader can do to build trust is to truly demonstrate interest and commitment to colleagues. The three C's each represent concepts that can deepen relationships quickly.

CARE

Caring means being curious about the people whom you work with. You have met many people who ask, "How are you doing?" and then walk away without waiting for an answer. This blatant disinterest is quickly recognized by colleagues. Make sure that, when you pay a social visit, you have the time and interest to listen well.

Memorize the names of family members, sports team affiliations, hobbies, pets and other interests. Make sure that you continue to ask about those things when you see the person the next time. In many European and South American countries, it is considered rude to get down to business without first asking questions about family and interests. Your genuine interest in learning about your colleagues as people will be greatly appreciated.

CONCERN

Concern means wanting input from colleagues and keeping up on issues that are important to them. It has to do with seeking them out and keeping them involved in critical decisions. This shows your colleagues that you want them to be successful.

Concern also is about offering help to people when they need/ask for it. When you show concern, you indicate that you are willing to spend time and effort to help others accomplish their goals. Whenever I have had the privilege of having support people to help me, I would often try to return the courtesy to them by offering my help when I had free time. If I had 15 minutes of time that was not allocated, I would always ask if I could assist them by bringing them coffee, changing light bulbs, getting copies from the copy machine or other small, but thoughtful activities.

COMPASSION

This deals with the emotional side of the relationship. When you show empathy and compassion, you seek to understand how others feel. You may not agree with their perceptions/feelings, but you demonstrate that you can see the world through their eyes. You reflect their feelings back to them when appropriate. They know that, if they are frustrated or hurting, you will be there to support them.

(NOTE: There is a fine line here when it comes to listening to "outside the workplace" issues. Since you are not a trained professional mental health worker, you don't want to get too deeply involved in "personal" matters. A referral to your EAP (Employee Assistance Program) or other mental health resource may be warranted. At times, when you listen to personal problems, your colleague may consider you to be their "friend" and expect treatment from you more as a "friend" than as a "leader." Even compassion has limits.)

2) ASK QUESTIONS

Leaders in various correctional and other paramilitary settings I have worked in are always surprised when I suggest that the mark of a great leader is the ability to ask the right questions of the right people at the right time. Their Common Sense notion is that becoming a leader means that you have reached a certain skill level and are now in a position to "tell" other people what is expected. Asking questions (particularly too many questions) is often perceived as a sign of uncertainty or even worse, weakness. Their sense is that you should know the answers.

The UnCommon Sense perspective suggests that there are many purposes for asking questions. Gathering information is only one part. Here are several other benefits of asking questions:

a) People see that you care about their opinion and input.
b) You have an opportunity to assess their perspective on how issues should be handled.
c) You can assess whether or not they see a broad enough range of options to solve problems.
d) You see how they frame/reframe problems.
e) You create more buy-in when decisions are made.
f) You allow for consensus decisions to be made as opposed to unilateral decisions.

g) You build trust because it shows that you are have not made decisions in isolation.

To enhance trust, ask for input in areas where you have not asked before. If done with sincerity, this truly demonstrates to your team that you value their input. However, don't ask questions if you truly don't want their input.

3) BE A GREAT LISTENER

Once you have asked a question, make sure you take the time and energy to listen, really listen. I watched a leader ask his group for their opinions and then promptly offer his own opinions before anyone else could respond. When other members spoke up, they essentially reinforced his views because they felt he did not really want to hear what they had to say. If you ask other people for their opinion, wait to give your ideas until they are done speaking. Show that you have heard what they have said.

There are 5 active listening skills that leaders should use:

a) Encouraging (Tell me more about that.)
b) Clarifying (Help me understand what you mean by that.)
c) Restating (What I hear you saying is...; repeat the facts.)
d) Reflecting (What I sense that you are feeling is...; repeat their feelings)
e) Summarizing (Recap the conversation.)

While they are all important, restating and reflecting are the most powerful to demonstrate good listening. Restating shows that you have accurately heard what they have said without twisting or changing any details. Reflecting shows that you have understood the accompanying feelings as well.

People who feel that they have been heard and understood are more likely to extend trust.

4) LEARN FROM OTHERS

Ask someone in the group to teach you how to do something. This should not be done in a patronizing manner. Make sure you sincerely want to learn the activity. Show appreciation for the time and effort your "teacher" takes in the instruction. The humility you show in being willing to become a student again is very powerful. Later, you will reverse roles and become their teacher.

When a new leader comes in, many employees are worried that she/he will come in and change many things BEFORE they understand what has been happening. Change will be accepted more readily when the leader seeks to understand what is going on BEFORE making significant changes.

5) SHARE YOUR TRUTH: THE LAWS OF SELF DISCLOSURE

When you are willing to tell people details about yourself, they will usually reciprocate in kind. Open up to your group by sharing (appropriate) previously unstated feelings or opinions. This will be viewed as a demonstration that you trust the group to handle all information, including difficult information.

Showing openness and vulnerability (not weakness) enhances feelings of trust. This is particularly true when men are willing to acknowledge sensitivity. I watched a two-star admiral in the Coast Guard address his staff following the tragic death of two individuals lost at sea. When he spoke, his voice cracked and tears ran down his face. He had to stop several times to compose himself. There was no doubt in anyone's mind that he cared deeply about the loss of those two men. The fact that he was willing to show his feelings openly made the grieving process that much more open for the entire group.

6) ASK FOR HELP

Own that you need "help" from your team/colleagues in several areas. This includes wanting to hear their feedback and thoughts. It also includes, wanting to hear their thoughts on potential options for solving problems. Additionally, it includes asking them to support your leadership, vision and strategy.

FEEDBACK

When a new leader comes in and makes changes, "pulse" needs to be taken to see how the changes are being implemented and received. When feedback only follows change of command channels, the feedback can get filtered. When a leader asks for feedback from many levels of employees, she/he is demonstrating interest in the perceptions of others.

People are more likely to extend trust to those who ask for their input.

OPTIONS

In discussing Option Thinking, always solicit at least three options:

    a) Best Case Scenario
    b) Worst Case Scenario
    c) Most Probable Case Scenario.

Option Thinking need not be limited to three options. Most people can process three to seven options simultaneously. As a leader, you should rarely accept a problem from anyone without gathering their input concerning options to remediate the issue.

Asking colleagues to bring multiple options along with problems engages them in the problem solving process. When you solve problems together, it builds trust, camaraderie and team spirit.

SUPPORT

Leaders can ask for support from everyone on the team. Rather than remain isolated as a leader, you solicit support for new goals and directions.

Support is not always unconditional and eternal, so it must be reinforced and rewarded whenever possible. You can say, "It makes my job so much easier when I know I have the support and backing of my staff." This models great leadership. The implication is that we have each other's' backs.

6) SHARE YOUR VISION

Create a vision for the next 30-90 days to show your team the direction that you are heading. Visions can definitely engender trust, if the vision is home grown and action driven.

Too many organizations have mission/vision and values statements from the Book of Mission and Vision Statements. They all sound and look the same. They deal in an ideal world that no one works in. They look good on paper but do not drive anyone's behavior. The average employee is unaware of what the vision is.

The best visions are ones that are grounded in the hearts and minds of the people involved. When Dr. Martin Luther King gave his famous "I Have a Dream" speech, it resonated with the audience because they shared his dream.

When Senior Management creates visions in isolation without input and buy-in from staff, the vision has little impact on trust. When the vision is created from the ground up and is intimately involved in everyday affairs, it matters more. I watched a CEO tell his employees that he was so focused on "customers" that he would leave any meeting any time the word customer was not used with great frequency. This let his employees know that he was quite serious about "customer focus."

When you commit yourself in thought and action to a set of ideas or principles that resonate with your employees, you build trust.

7) CELEBRATE SMALL SUCCESSES

Celebrate small successes with the team; don't just wait for major milestones. Share in the celebration of inch stones and foot stones. When leaders are willing to take time out from their busy schedules to shine the spotlight on the team during initial steps, it validates that everyone is important.

Think: When was the last time your Senior Management team celebrated the harvest of easily accomplished activities ("low hanging fruit"?) People appreciate the personal recognition and this creates further buy in for the long run.

8) CREATE OPPORTUNITIES FOR OTHERS TO BE SUCCESSFUL

This fits under the heading of giving people a chance to shine in front of their peers. I worked with a brilliant financial analyst, Sonia, who was incredibly uncomfortable stepping up and making a presentation in front of Senior Management. She felt uncomfortable that they might spot an error in her work or ask her a question that she couldn't answer. Creating a "safe" environment was critical to helping Sonia.

Sonia was given an opportunity to speak in front of a group of "friendly" middle managers first about a topic that she was certain about. Questions were limited to the tail end of the presentation. Additionally, I offered to help her if tough questions were asked.

Sonia did very well and was slowly groomed for the "main stage." By the time she made a presentation to Senior Management, she was confident in her work and looked forward to the opportunity. The trust relationship between us was enhanced because I attempted to guarantee her success using SSPS (three successes in a row.)

9) PUT THE GROUP FIRST

Whenever an opportunity presents itself, choose the option that benefits the group/department instead of the option that benefits you. Shining the spotlight on others is an indication of humility. When credit is deserved, the great leader always acknowledges the contributions of others. If financial rewards are available, make sure everyone gets to participate in those rewards.

10) TALK ABOUT TRUST

Create an open environment to talk about trust. Deal with it openly and encourage others to do so. Make it a regular agenda item and address:

a) The current level of trust
b) What is contributing to that level of trust
c) What can be done to enhance trust

Trust is such a pivotal issue that it often underlies other problems. During my 30 years as a coach and consultant, I have seen that issues concerning trust and disrespect are the most frequent causes of unrest and turbulence in organizations. While people may want to discuss the surface issues because they are more "factual," the reality is that if the trust and or disrespect issue was addressed, the "factual" issue would all but disappear. Modeling the idea that trust is a good and necessary topic of conversation will build trust.

11) TRUST OTHERS FIRST

Leaders are willing to extend trust to those people who they feel most comfortable with. This does not mean that they trust indiscriminately. I understand that people with "street smarts" may be uncomfortable with this idea. However, prudently trusting another person's choices, information and preferences can accelerate the trust relationship.

Extending your trust beyond what others are willing to do may demonstrate trust in a practical way. We tend to trust those that trust us. Demonstrate that you are willing to expand the parameters of your trust for team/department members. Identify the criteria you will use to do so. Publicly acknowledge team members when they expand their trust horizons. Praise them for helping to build trust in the group.

12) ADMIT YOUR ERRORS

If errors have occurred (regardless of fault) or perceptions about your behavior are negative, publicly acknowledge the errors, behavior or perception and show contrition. If there is any heat to be taken, share that with the team. Always be willing to accept your share of the responsibility. While some people may be interested in why these behaviors occurred, more will be interested in your desire to accept responsibility.

Some leaders feel that admitting an error causes a drop in credibility. As long as there are no fatal errors, admitting a few of them actually enhances credibility. I was witness to a dramatic display of this when a CEO stood up at an annual meeting, cracked an egg on his head and said, "I have egg on my face because of decisions I made last year that did not help the company."

13) ACHIEVE ATONEMENT: BECOMING "AT ONE"

Once we have acknowledged an issue with a past behavior, we need to show rededication to becoming "at one" with others and with the mission. Sacrificing time, energy and/or effort for your team/department attests to the sincerity of your acknowledgement. This models the way for others.

When people are not successful in accomplishing a key task, they can pout and sulk. They may seek to affix the blame on others.

Great leaders show increased determination to do better. They study what they did and did not do, seek new options and put in the hard work to do better.

14) ACCEPT THE LEARNING CURVE: NO ONE IS PERFECT

Admitting that you are not perfect and feel the need to work on elements of your leadership also engenders trust in others. It models that everyone should be on a continuous improvement campaign. Building on the strengths that they have, leaders can reach out to others and ask them to step up. Employees can feel confident when they ask for coaching and mentorship, trusting that it will be viewed in a positive manner.

When trust falters, acknowledge the issue and seek to understand the factors that have caused the trust disconnects. Recommit to do better.

Remember that it is very hard, if not impossible, to maintain high trust all of the time with every person; however, doing the hard work and following UnCommon Sense makes it more likely to maintain most of the time.

THOUGHT BOMBS TO CONSIDER:

1) How much time and effort have you put in to building trust with your colleagues?
2) Which of the strategies mentioned have you used? Which have worked? Which strategies need tweaking?
3) Which new strategies hold promise for you in your work environment? Which would be the easiest for you to implement?
4) Think about your organization. Is it a high trust environment? Is trust openly discussed? How can you encourage conversation about trust?
5) If you have a trust disconnect with any of your colleagues, which strategies are you willing to consider in order improving the trust relationship?

CHAPTER 19

CAREFRONTATION VS. CONFRONTATION

COMMON SENSE

When there are issues, it is best to face them directly and factually. It is also necessary to speak to the other party directly. Letting others know what is bothering you is an essential part of leadership. Too many people sweep their issues under the rug, instead of dealing with them head on.

UNCOMMON SENSE

Every issue has an emotional and a logical side. If emotional issues are not dealt with first in a safe, positive and supportive manner, it may be difficult to agree on the logical issues and the resolutions to those issues. Additionally, many people have difficulty separating their feelings about the conflicted issues and their feelings about the other party.

Consider the following situation:

Santo was a brilliant engineer in charge of a large project. He had two other engineers working with him on the project. He trusted Hugo implicitly. Arthur, on the other hand, had made several critical errors recently and had fallen out of favor with Santo. Being an engineer, Santo did not tell this directly to Arthur. Since his typical mode of communication was "telepathy," he instead started acting differently towards Arthur. Arthur knew something was up, but he never asked Santo about it. He did talk to Hugo and anyone else who would listen about his feeling that "something was not right." When I asked Santo why he didn't come right out and share his feelings with Arthur, he offered the following excuses at different times:

1) Arthur was easily excitable and might quit. If he quit, there was no guarantee that Santo would be able fill his spot with another head count.
2) Arthur might react emotionally and who knows what he could do.
3) Arthur wasn't that bad; he just made a few mistakes. Hopefully, if Arthur was reassigned to "easier" work, he would realize that he would have to work harder if he wanted his old work back again.
4) Arthur was a bright guy. He would figure out what was wrong and do something about it.
5) It might hurt Arthur's feelings.

The bottom line was that Santo and Arthur were both fairly typical engineers and "confrontation phobic." Neither one of them wanted to discuss the issue openly. Santo was engaging in a classic case of "LBP" (Leadership by Praying, wishing and hoping that things would get better without either one of them having to really do much of anything.)

Just starting the conversation is difficult enough. Most technical people would begin this "CONfrontation" with Engineer A "telling" Engineer B:

1) The issues with B's work
2) Why B's behavior was causing problems (in an almost accusatory manner)
3) That interactions between A and B were uncomfortable.

This strategy will almost certainly create a feeling of ambush in Engineer B. At this point, without consciously realizing it, Engineer B will become instantly defensive to protect against his/her sense of attack. Many technical people have great difficulty separating criticism of the problem from personal criticism.

Let's remember that, in this kind of situation, there are as many emotional issues as there are logic issues. The interaction will go much more smoothly if the emotional issues are addressed first.

"Telling" your counterpart what you believe are the "facts" is the Common Sense approach to solving this problem. UnCommon Sense suggests that there are two sets of facts (one for each person). Additionally, remember that the facts are not what is the most critical. It is the perceptions of those facts by both individuals that must be reconciled. Therefore, rather than "telling" each other anything, you might open up the conversation with several of the following questions:

1) Are we doing OK?
2) Do you feel like I am treating you in the same way as I have in the past?
3) Are you feeling uncomfortable about anything?
4) How do you feel about our working relationship?
5) Is this a good time to talk about a few things?

The purpose of these questions is to:

1) Calibrate your counterpart's interest and awareness of any issues
2) Begin to create a "safe" space, so that a positive CAREfrontation can occur
3) Calibrate the willingness to discuss feelings
4) Evaluate how strongly the other person feels and how guarded they are against having this conversation
5) Assure that the person has the time and willingness to talk about the situation right now.

CAREfrontation is a process that I have developed to help you to join with the other person to deal with the problem. The other person is not the problem. The problem is the problem. If you can join with your counterpart and attack the problem together, there will be less need to attack each other. It is critical to create a "safe" space where both parties feel that they can speak openly without fear of retribution or repercussions. It is equally critical that both parties have mutual respect for one another, a common goal and a willingness to solve the problem. These guidelines can be established as part of the "E & B" conversation discussed in Chapter 17.

The key tools used in CAREfrontation are:

LISTENING

It is critical to listen with interest and curiosity when the other person is speaking. This process uses active listening skills insofar as you are listening in order to understand more than you are listening to respond and defend. You are simply gathering information. You are also listening to understand the perception of the other party. Are they seeing the issue from the same vantage point? How can understanding both perspectives help both parties to find common ground?

EMPATHY

There is a big difference between empathy and sympathy. Sympathy means that you are feeling the other person's pain. Empathy means that you have the ability to understand their concerns and communicate them back to the other person. It also involves being able to see the situation from the other person's point of view. It involves being responsive to any sense of fear, hurt or disrespect that the other person may be experiencing.

QUESTIONS

CAREfrontation involves asking questions so that both participants' stories/views/ opinions can be brought out into the open. There will be less need to argue about the "facts" of the situation if each person has a better understanding of the others' point of view

It is very helpful if, AFTER each person has shared his/her view of the story, that the following agreements can be offered.

There may NOT be agreement about:

1) who is to blame in this situation. (In any 2-person problem, each person bears some responsibility. It may not be 50/50, but it is also not likely to be 90/10. There may be situational,

political, economic or other idiosyncratic factors impacting the situation as well.)

2) who started the situation
3) who got hurt/disrespected more
4) the "facts" of the situation.

There can be agreement that:

5) no one likes to feel hurt/disrespected
6) if behavior continues in the same manner, the hurt feelings will continue
7) doing nothing will not solve the problem
8) if mutual purpose is defined/ clarified and mutual respect is demonstrated, more palatable options can be found.

Using the LENSA Model and CAREfrontation can turn many of these "non-versations" into conversations. Imagine if Santo and Arthur had been able to hold this type of conversation. Their situation could have been dealt with in a more optimal manner.

THOUGHT BOMBS TO CONSIDER:

1) In the midst of a heated discussion, can help to create a safe space?
2) When you are upset with someone, can you slow your reactions down to hear their story and concerns?
3) Do you have the need to be right (even if it prolongs the discussion and delays finding a mutually acceptable solution?) What drives that need?
4) Can you separate your feelings about the situation from your feelings about the other person?
5) Can you collaborate with someone that you disagree with?

CHAPTER 20

SUGGESTION CAMPAIGNS THAT WORK

COMMON SENSE

It is a great idea to get employees involved in making suggestions for improvement. In order to show true openness, it is important to give employees every opportunity to make suggestions about any topic that matters to them at any time. Putting up suggestion boxes in several areas around the company will give all employees the opportunity to participate.

UNCOMMON SENSE

Many suggestion programs have failed due to lack of trust or lack of feedback given during previous suggestion campaigns. Reinvigorating your suggestion program may require energy, excitement and a few tweaks to what you are currently doing.

One measure of an engaged workforce is the willingness to make suggestions to improve productivity/efficiency or to save costs. Apathetic or jaded employees treat suggestion programs as an opportunity to gripe about issues that irritate them. Engaged employees view suggestion programs as an opportunity to become part of the solution. Engaged employees feel empowered and feel that their contributions are valuable and will be considered.

In the 1990's, there was a trend towards "empowering employees." Numerous companies embarked upon empowerment campaigns as a means of coping with economic downturns and reductions in force that were prevalent during that decade.

Typical empowerment campaigns were based on the following concepts:

1) In a "do more with less" environment, decisions that had been previously made by Senior Management had to be delegated to lower level employees in order to save money. The cost of approving a $500 budgeted expenditure almost doubled when Senior Management had to spend their time and energy making the decision. Companies began to try to reduce the number of people involved in the signature cycle as a way to lower the cost and speed up the decision. After all, why should it take more than one person to approve the purchase of an inexpensive, previously budgeted item?

2) Employees who had not been given raises might appreciate what they perceived as greater span of control in terms of more responsibility on their job. (This notion may be true for Average Plus employees and some Water Walkers but may not be true for the 3 other categories of employees.) Expanding employees' horizons might also sensitize them to what was going on around them. Employees who are not empowered often take a myopic view of the world, simply focusing themselves on their own work. They tend not to see/care much about what is impacting colleagues above and below them.

3) Employees might become more promotable when "the good times" returned because they had expanded the scope of their job. The reality or illusion of a faster career track was dangled in front of employees as an incentive to accept empowerment.

4) Micro management was out, and delegation was in. Unfortunately, this often meant that Senior Management "dumped" unwanted work on employees without involving them in the decision of what to delegate. Employees who felt that they could choose some of what was delegated to them might have been a bit more receptive to that delegation.

5) Generation "X" employees starting leaving their jobs more frequently than had previous generations when they thought they had learned everything that the job offered. To keep those employees engaged, expanding the scope of their job could conceivably prolong their careers within an

organization. Unfortunately, the reasons for Gen X's limited loyalty were rarely explored and addressed.

6) With the advent and emergence of quality programs, employees were all invited to participate in the continuous improvement cycle as members of Quality Improvement Teams (QITs).

All of these concepts and the accompanying logic were sound. Then why did most empowerment programs routinely fail? The answer is fairly simple.

Empowerment is as much an emotional issue as it is a logical issue. Companies rarely sought to preface empowerment programs with programs designed to energize their employees. Employees who had seen layoffs, restructuring and reorganizations throughout the 1980's and 1990's began to limit the loyalty they were willing to show their organizations. If organizations were quick to rid themselves of "extra" employees during down times, why should employees step above and beyond expectations to help their organizations? Empowerment campaigns were perceived as "a lot more work without additional compensation or chance for promotion." These programs were not likely to engage or energize the majority of the workforce.

Neither money nor effort was spent to reassure employees of their value and to get them excited about the "short term vision" and plan for the organization. Employees were not placed in the inner communication loop of the organization where they could see a long term path for themselves. Worst of all, employees were not "asked" to contribute extra effort. They were "told" to contribute extra effort. Without meaning, additional appreciation, compensation and or promotion, empowerment never had a chance.

In the 1990's, Tom Peters conducted a global study to identify the level of *suggestion giving* in major corporations and found a clear difference in the expectation involved between Japanese corporations and American corporations. Clearly, the expectation for suggestion giving is far more rooted in Japanese corporations, where it has become a significant part of their corporate culture. The difference in terms of the number of suggestions received by corporations was staggering.

According to Peters, the best corporation in the world at suggestion generation in the mid 1990's was Matsushita Electronics (the manufacturer of Panasonic Seiko and other major brands of electronic equipment.) During one calendar year, they received more than 6.5 million suggestions from their workforce. Even though they are a very large corporation, it broke down to approximately 75-80 suggestions per employee per year.

Breaking it down further, they received approximately 6 suggestions per employee per month. The implementation rate for suggestions was close to 75%, so the final breakdown was that they received approximately 1 implementable suggestion per employee per week. Amazing.

Now that was the best corporation. How about the average Japanese corporation?

The average Japanese corporation received about 25 suggestions per employee per year. That breaks down to approximately 2 suggestions per employee per month. Implementation rates were a bit lower, but the bottom line was that they still received between 1 and 1 ½ implementable suggestions per month. Not too bad, particularly when you compare that number with the average American corporation.

American corporations received approximately 1 suggestion for every 40 employees per year with an implementation rate of closer to 25%. That means that American corporations receive one implementable suggestion for every 150 employees per year. Not a good sign.

For most of the 1990's, I offered a variety of ideas centered on the idea of "Energizing the Workplace" to help boost the number and quality of suggestions received. I was asked to make a presentation at a service awards banquet in Indiana. This corporation manufactured parts for automotive vehicle exhaust systems. There is a good chance that you have a piece of their equipment installed on your vehicle right now.

One award presented at the banquet was to a group of individuals working within the same department who had generated almost ONE SUGGESTION PER EMPLOYEE PER DAY for ONE MONTH. What?

I was astonished. I asked to speak with the supervisor of the group to find out how they had accomplished this unheard of feat. You might wonder which department the suggestions had come from. Engineering? Sales? Customer Service? Marketing? Operations? Actually, it was none of the above. The suggestions came from the Maintenance Department shortly after they had been visited and personally asked to do so by the COO of the corporation.

Remember Rusty on his first day at the airline? He had personally gone to the maintenance department seeking their input. As with Rusty's visit, this other corporation's COO's visit had little to do with the department (with all due respect to maintenance departments.) It had much more to do with the personal nature of the "call to help." When employees saw that Senior Management was willing to visit with them in their work area, appreciate their work and then ask for needed suggestions, the request was perceived in a more positive manner. When employees believe that Senior Management is sincerely interested and responsive to their suggestions, then suggestions are made in earnest.

How many times have you seen suggestion programs which are kicked off with an email? No personal visit. No personal plea. Just an email.

How often have you made suggestions and received no acknowledgement or feedback about the suggestion? You are kept in the dark as to whether or not the suggestion was on target or not. I can't imagine that this would encourage you to offer additional suggestions.

If you would like to increase the number and quality of the suggestions that you receive by 200%-400%, I offer the following guidelines which I developed as a review of suggestion programs across the country. While I can't guarantee the results for every organization, the following activities will increase your likelihood of success:

1) A personal appeal from the CEO, COO or significant advocate inside the organization explaining the need for suggestions. This should be preceded by an acknowledgement of the past, present and anticipated significant contributions of the work force.
2) A description of the short-term vision for the organization (a 90-day plan) and how the suggestion program can help the organization actualize the vision.
3) A commitment by the organization to consider all suggestions and to offer feedback to all suggestion givers.

(Note: At 3M, it was traditional to offer occasional awards for the "Worst Suggestions" offered. The point of this was not to mock unusual suggestions. It was to honor the idea that all suggestions were valuable, even if they were not immediately accepted. 3M has a history of finding value in seemingly failed ideas. Just because a suggestion was not accepted at first did not mean that it might not stimulate someone else at a later time to get up and run with it.)

4) A minimal reward/recognition campaign to honor everyone who participated in the program.

The following 7 ideas can provide the framework for your new suggestion program:

1) Short-term Campaigns
2) One Goal At A Time
3) Personal Benefit Before Organizational Benefit
4) Ask ONLY What You Are Willing To Change
5) Suggestions Evaluated By SEC's (Suggestion Evaluations Committees)
6) All Suggestions Get Rapid Feedback

7) Implemented Suggestions Are Publicized And Rewarded.

Consider these ideas in more detail:

SHORT-TERM CAMPAIGNS

When organizations put suggestion boxes up and keep them up year round, the boxes rarely serve their intended purpose. They often become repositories for garbage or for gripes about ongoing issues. Too often, management only finds suggestions to increase wages and benefits for rank and file, while decreasing wages and benefits for Senior Management. Senior Management quickly becomes disenchanted with hearing these suggestions repeatedly, and the programs die from disuse. At best, suggestion boxes are seen as part of the furnishings of the office and are routinely ignored.

The critical point is that no sense of urgency is created during ongoing suggestion programs. Employees do not put "Make a suggestion" on their "To Do" lists. It becomes one of those low-level tasks that they never get around to.

You are more likely to have success when you run time-limited, short-term suggestion programs that run approximately 4-6 weeks. This leaves adequate time for an employee to make a suggestion, get feedback and then resubmit the suggestion. When there is no deadline for receiving suggestions, other deadline-based priorities often take precedence.

There is no hard and fast rule about the duration of the program. It is a PENZON, which means it depends on the situation, depends on the size of the organization, depends on the complexity of the suggestion program, etc.

ONE GOAL AT A TIME

Employees are more likely to make suggestions when there is a clear target and goal. Having one goal brings focus to suggestions. The goal can be broad such as how to rearrange equipment or office furniture to make it more workable. When there is one goal, it is easier for the SECs to create common criteria that they can use to evaluate all suggestions side by side. When suggestions are given about a wide variety of topics, it can be the equivalent of comparing apples to oranges.

It is important that the campaign and the evaluation process be open and transparent to everyone. Employees will have more faith in the validity of the program if they have the right and ability to view all suggestions and the criteria that were used to evaluate them. In the long run, suggestion evaluation programs can be used to build/ rebuild trust between rank and file and Senior Management. The clearer the messaging about the program, the greater the likelihood of success (particularly when coupled with the other steps).

PERSONAL BENEFIT BEFORE ORGANIZATIONAL BENEFIT

When organizations embark upon suggestion campaigns, they make one mistake more often than any other. They ask for suggestions concerning a major issue that is strictly for the benefit of the organization. Employees who may be wary of the motivations behind suggestion programs are yet again asked to reach down and help the organization instead of being allowed and encouraged to help themselves. Additionally, complex organizational issues often require complex suggestions, and it is important to have easy, initial successes to reestablish the program as viable.

To ensure success, it is helpful to ask for suggestions about an area of concern to employees. This should be coupled with sincere statements concerning appreciation for all the hard work that has already being accomplished. This opening gambit shows that Senior Management recognizes and appreciates their employees and wants to exert energy and effort towards meeting employee satisfaction. Typical first suggestion programs can involve asking for suggestions on any of the following issues:

1) celebratory events (e.g., company picnics, outings and holiday parties)

2) the purchase of equipment/furniture for break rooms
3) food to add to/remove from the menu in the cafeteria
4) ways to enhance social interaction between groups/ departments
5) ways to enhance upstream/downstream or interdepartmental communication

ASK ONLY WHAT YOU ARE WILLING TO CHANGE

Another common error is to ask for suggestions in areas where you have little or no interest/ability in making changes. Nothing frustrates employees more than being asked for a suggestion and then being told that nothing can be done about it. Why bother to ask the question in the first place if the answer is a guaranteed "NO"?

Don't ask questions about job satisfaction, wages or benefits if you have no intention of changing anything about them. It is also important to ask questions where there are a variety of possible options. Asking a question that naturally leads to just one conclusion can also be frustrating.

In the early stages of establishing/reestablishing a suggestion program, it is critical to ask a question that pleasantly surprises employees by demonstrating Senior Management flexibility in an area where there was no perceived flexibility. Good examples of this might include asking employees to identify:

1) redundancy in reports and metrics
2) "red tape" obstacles that can be reduced or eliminated
3) policies and procedures that are no longer useful
4) meetings that can be shortened or combined
5) methods to simplify work functions

Careful thought must be applied to the wording and range of suggestions solicited. This is to ensure that the widest possible array of suggestions that may be included in the program. Senior Management does not lose control over the process because limitations can be placed on the scope of suggestions requested.

However, if the limitations are viewed as too restrictive, the number of suggestions may decline as well.

SUGGESTIONS ARE EVALUATED BY SUGGESTION EVALUATION COMMITTEES (SEC's)

In order to restore credibility to the suggestion program process, it is critical that Senior Management turn over the evaluation process to a group of SEC's. As previously stated, Senior Management may input limitations concerning evaluation criteria, cost, time line and other relevant data, but the ultimate decisions to adopt or reject suggestions should be left to the SEC's, which will be held accountable for their actions.

SEC's should be composed of a small number of individuals (typically 3-5) to ensure rapid feedback and decision making. An odd number of people is preferable to avoid stalemates. The SEC's should have time limited terms of service (usually less than 1 year, which provides continuity and fluidity.)

The composition of the first SEC is important. Find volunteers who are willing and able to judge suggestions. They must be given time to participate in the review. Picking Average Plus employees is always a temptation, but you should realize that many of them are already overburdened with heavy workloads. It would not be advised to select chronic complainers or employees with low credibility either because the first SEC groups will be carefully scrutinized to make sure that they are fair, open and capable of making reasonable decisions. Early groups will be judged on their objectivity in dealing with suggestions.

Often when the screening process is not conducted carefully, the SEC's are accused of "favoritism" in accepting and rejecting suggestions.

ALL SUGGESTIONS GET RAPID FEEDBACK

What frustrates most well-intended suggestion givers is not hearing any feedback about their ideas. When little or no feedback is offered, suggestion givers either feel that they were ignored or that the suggestion program is a front for Senior Management to do what they wanted to do all along. In very few cases is feedback ever offered face-to-face.

Evaluators are often concerned that there will be a negative backlash when suggestions are rejected or modifications to the suggestions are requested. However, imagine your delight if you made a suggestion, knew what the evaluation criteria were, and then received direct feedback from a member of the SEC in a positive manner.

In a previous chapter, I offered advice on how to CAREfront difficult situations. CAREfronting suggestion feedback should reduce the likelihood of unpleasant feedback sessions. When feedback is given openly and honestly, it enhances long-term communications.

The goal would be for a member of the SEC to meet with each person who offers a suggestion within one to two weeks and inform them of the feedback from the SEC. This is a huge PENZON (It depends on the situation). Here are several of the factors that will help you to determine the reasonableness of the timeframe for feedback:

1) the size of the company
2) the number of suggestions received
3) the number of SEC's reviewing suggestions
4) how often the SEC's meet to review suggestions
5) the complexity of the question asked
6) the training of SEC members to provide constructive feedback.

In the long run, it would be more advantageous to provide good solid feedback, even if the length of the suggestion program had to be extended. If the feedback is given within 3 weeks, it will still be appreciated as long as the quality of the feedback is high. Word will quickly spread throughout the organization when people feel that they are being fairly heard.

IMPLEMENTED SUGGESTIONS ARE PUBLICIZED AND REWARDED

This step creates good will for the long-term sustenance of the program. It validates the idea that the request for suggestions was sincere and shows appreciation to employees who participate. It shows that Senior Management values the suggestions and is willing to back up that appreciation with symbolic or financial rewards.

Different people may want different rewards for making strong suggestions. In fact, this can be one of the first suggestion programs -- asking employees how they would like to be rewarded within the scope of budget available. Some people might prefer public recognition. Others would prefer a picture in the company newsletter. Others might prefer a discrete thank you. One size does not fit all when it comes to rewards and publicity. Remember that a reward is not a reward unless the person receiving it perceives it is a reward.

Rewards and publicity must be changed regularly if the program gets traction. Most reward programs have a shelf life of one to two years. After that, the rewards are either considered routine, expected or unimportant.

Think of the number of paper certificates given out by your organization each year. How many of the recipients of these symbolic gestures truly appreciate them? Put as much care into the rewards and publicity as you put in for all the other steps. This step should not be viewed as gravy but more as an integral ingredient in the overall success of the suggestion program.

Combining all of these steps, accompanied by Senior Management acknowledgement and good will, can go a long way to increasing dramatically the number of suggestions you receive.

THOUGHT BOMBS TO PONDER:

1) Do you currently have a functioning employee suggestion program in place? How many suggestions do you receive annually? What is the caliber of those suggestions? How many are implemented?

2) Has Senior Management acknowledged employee contributions? Do they conduct LBWA visits?

3) Do employees regularly receive feedback about suggestions that they make? From whom? Do they receive acknowledgement for suggestions that are implemented?

4) Are employees rewarded for making suggestions? Do they value the rewards that they receive?

5) In what areas would you most benefit from employee suggestions?

CHAPTER 21

THRIVING DURING CONSTANT CHANGE

COMMON SENSE

Change is a logical process that can be planned. You need to understand the factors that are driving the change and then you will be able to accept it.

UNCOMMON SENSE

Change is an emotional event that stirs up deep seated feelings. If you are energized and optimistic about having more options as a result of the changes, you will be more likely to accept it.

Change is the only constant. Do you like things the way they are? Too bad. Just wait a while, and things will change. Things may evolve or devolve. They may become simpler or more complex. The reality is that you just can't become complacent and expect things to remain the same because few, if any, things remain the same. Not people. Not technology. Not much.

When I ask audiences who likes change, half of the audience usually raises their hands. When I then ask who loves change, hands start to drop. When I complete the trilogy and ask who likes chaos, only the hearty remain. I usually tell the audience that they are all basically liars. As they start to protest, I explain why I have called them liars.

Think about this yourself. On most days, from the time you wake up and wipe drool off the side of your chin till you leave the house, you have a predictable, comfortable routine that you follow religiously. You find yourself doing things exactly in the same order day after day. If you have children who need to get off to school this is a must.

You follow that up by driving exactly the same way to get to work each day. You have figured out the best way to get to work (even knowing which lanes to stay in and which lanes to avoid between certain highway exits). No reason to fool around about it.

When you are driving on the highway, anyone driving slower than you are is an idiot and anyone driving faster than you are is a maniac. Of course, you are the official speed on the road. You wonder why the traffic folks don't just call you up each morning to check with you to see how fast you will be driving to work on that particular day so they can let the other drivers know. But I digress.

Life without some semblance of structure and predictability would be quite different. Living in the "here and now" involves being able to see each event and activity as if it were a new event or activity. Watch the joy that a baby brings to seeing things for the first time. There is genuine amazement in their eyes as they try to take it all in. While it would be hard to do every single activity differently each day, you could do ONE thing differently each day. That is one of the true secrets to thriving during change.

People who thrive on change practice making changes BEFORE they have to so that, when they have to, they know how to. Change involves learning how to deal with the discomfort of not knowing what will happen.

In general, people love changes that increase the number of options that they have. You would be happy if you received a raise, a promotion or went on vacation because these events increase your choices.

They are less excited about changes that decrease the number of options that they have. You would be unhappy if you were fired, demoted or had your home burglarized.

The trick is to view any change as being filled with endless possibilities. Think of change like a candy store. If you love candy, the biggest problem will be which candy to buy. You can't really go wrong since you like so many different kinds.

For years, I used to have a trademarked button that looked like this:

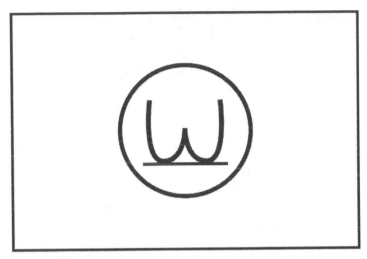

Diagram 4

I asked people to guess what the button represented. Some people thought it had something to do with George W. Bush during the years that he was the President. Since he wasn't my favorite President, that wasn't what I was looking for.

Others turned their heads to the side and thought it looked like the number "31." Others began to think about parts of the female anatomy. None of these guesses were correct. I finally stated that it was a "Put Your Butt on the Line" button. If I were to ask you if you put your butt on the line every day at work, most of you would say yes.

Here is my definition of putting your butt on the line. How many of you can tell me that you do/learn about/try at least 1 thing that you have never done each and every day? If you were willing to spend just 15 minutes a day learning something new, trying something out, researching a new idea, imagine how you would feel about change.

The more change you experience, the easier it gets. If change becomes a part of your day every day, then when you have to change something, you will know how to go about it.

Here are some funny things to try to get you to begin to laugh at the prospect of change:

1) Walk into a restaurant and when the hostess asks if you have reservations, tell her, "Yes, but I came anyway."
2) Before the waiter/waitress can say anything to you, offer them your name and tell them you will be their customer tonight.
3) Go into a photo studio and offer to buy pictures of the other people.
4) Wear two different types of shoes to work.
5) Go to Sea World carrying a fishing pole and ask, "Where is Shamu at?"

There is a serious message behind this silliness. When you read these suggestions, you may have felt that you weren't willing to do those things. You probably felt uneasy. You may have felt that you would be embarrassed to act in such an out of the ordinary mode.

All of those feelings are perfectly reasonable. THE IRONY IS THAT IS EXACTLY THE WAY WE FEEL EVERY TIME WE ARE ASKED TO MAKE A CHANGE. Awkward. Uncertain. Frightened at the prospect of looking foolish or being unsuccessful. That is exactly why we need to practice making changes so we can master getting past those feelings.

The model of change that I find helpful suggests that people go through 4 stages when they make most changes. The model is as follows:

Stage 1: Denial (We don't need to make no stinkin' changes.)

Stage 2: Anger/Hurt (Why do I have to be the one who has to change?)

Stage 3: Option Thinking (What choices do I have?)

Stage 4: Action (Let's get on with it.)

There are several ideas embedded in this model that you should consider. The first major issue is that the first 2 stages of change deal with the emotional side of change.

As with most workplace challenges, change has both an emotional and logical side. As I previously mentioned regarding communications and conflict resolution, you will find it easier to deal with change if you address the emotional side before you address the logical side.

Most people want to just jump into change and decide what options they have, ignoring the emotional blocks that delay change. If you don't deal with the emotional issues first, they will continue to creep back into the process until you deal with them. For most people, the main issue is dealing with fear of failure or fear of acting awkward. That is why the reaction most people have when facing the need to change is straight up denial.

DENIAL

Denial is the first stage of change for most people. When people are faced with the need for change, they suddenly turn Egyptian because they start living in Denial (De Nile). Sorry for the pun.

Why is denial the most typical reaction to the need for change? When a change in your behavior is required, it seems like a new and totally foreign situation even if it has been staring you right in the face for awhile. Denial provides your brain (consciously and/or unconsciously) with time to begin to search for options. Sometimes you hope for a "do over" or "mulligan" so you don't have to face the issue. This is an emotional reaction, not a logical reaction. At the core, denial is about feeling unsafe and being concerned with failure or other consequences. Ultimately when you feel "safe," you will consider other responses.

When I was 51 years old, I had 2 heart attacks, 10 weeks apart. That sounds like a fairly good reason to consider diet, exercise, sleep and work regimen changes. Considering that 40% of men do not get up from a heart attack, I should have felt fortunate that I was one of the 60% who survived.

After the first heart attack, I didn't know what to think. After all, it happened so quickly. I only had one blockage in one spot in one artery. I tasted some recommended healthier foods but found them unpalatable. I remember saying that I would rather die than have to change my diet to eat only these foods.

I did not recognize that I was in denial. I had never had to deal with an event like that before. Having the heart attack suddenly demanded quick and decisive behavior change. I did not take my medication with the regularity required. I eliminated some foods but not all of the foods that were unhealthy.

It took the second heart attack to really get my attention. After that, I got the message. Although I was angry that this had happened to me at a comparably young age, I proceeded to change my diet, exercise and work regimens. Some of us are just slow learners.

ANGER

The second stage of change involves dealing with your anger and hurt about having to make a change. During this phase, you may feel angry. You begin to resent the fact that you have to change. You fantasize about others having to change, while you remain in your present state.

Don't be fooled by your anger. Anger is the external manifestation of hurt. Hurt is the real feeling that underlies your anger. You feel frightened, embarrassed or even ashamed at having to acknowledge the need for change. You are frightened of failure as well. You keep wishing, hoping and praying that something else will happen that will eliminate the need for change.

A lot of "What If's" come to mind at this point. Your brain is just searching for a way to adjust in a successful manner. All of the emotional turmoil that you feel is just an opportunity to buy time and delay the inevitable change.

Another point to consider is that the reason people stay in the first 2 stages for too long is because they are uncomfortable about having to alter their safe and trusted routines. When do people get divorced? The answer is TOO LATE. When do people leave jobs that they hate? The answer is TOO LATE. When do people do something positive to correct health issues? The answer is TOO LATE.

See a pattern here? Many people, even faced with misery, unhappiness and illness, will still hold out for "magical intervention" as a better course of behavior than active change. Our angry feelings cause us to wish, hope and pray that other people will make changes so that we will not have to. This is not a logical process. It is rooted in fears of the unknown. Until you face up to the obstacles you have, it will be tough to commit wholeheartedly to behavioral change.

In the corporate world, staying in the first two stages of change creates a lack of "corporate agility." Agility is defined as the ability to shift resources from areas of low ROI (Return On Investment) to areas of higher ROI and is a critical issue today. Agility is what allows "disruptive technology" to level the playing field.

Organizations that have existed with silos are far less maneuverable than organizations that operate cross functionally. Organizations with long standing traditions find it hard to adjust to changes in the world. Monopolies such as the post office, telephone and utilities have been among the slower movers. When they were the only game in town, they changed slowly. Once competition was allowed onto the playing field, major adjustments had to be made.

I don't think the post office ever foresaw the impact that email would have on their business model. If they had seen it, you might not see Fed Ex boxes sitting in front of their structures today. I have given presentations to many fire and police organizations where I have complimented them on "boldly marching into the 20th century." Too bad we are in the 21st century.

Think about it. How stuck are you or your organization in your ways? How many ideas do you import from the outside? A recent study suggested that great companies were constantly looking at best practices in their industry and related industries in order to import ideas from the outside. One guru speculated that 50% of all ideas should originate from outside the organization. Is it any wonder that hospitals are looking at the best practices of hotels? Are you surprised at how many companies send their customer service people to study with the "Imagineers" at Disneyland?

The answer lies in identifying obstacles and old scripts as quickly as possible to clear the way for dealing with the logical side of change. One tool to use has already been detailed in the chapter about the 5 different types of employees. In discussing how to motivate Average Minus employees, I offered several examples of SSPS (Successful Sequential Problem Solving.) The same concept applies here. Building on small successes goes a long way to help overcome fears of failure and awkwardness.

OPTION THINKING

The third stage of change, entitled Option Thinking, begins the more logical aspect of dealing with change. Once you have dealt with the emotional barriers to making change, you can move on to considering options. Once the need for change is accepted, options can be identified and action can begin.

I do not mean to minimize the challenge of finding the right options, preparing employees for the changes and effectively implementing them. But compared to the emotional blocks, they are more straightforward to deal with.

When it comes to dealing with the logical side to change, I have introduced the concept of Option Thinking. Too often when people are faced with the need for change, they quickly focus on tried and true methods from the past.

This is neither right nor wrong. It is simply how logical people first seek to solve a problem. If it worked well in the past, why not just stay with it? If it ain't broke, don't fix it. A more novel approach was offered by Robert Kriegel, who suggested, "If it ain't broke, break it.' as a way to encourage novel thinking. Here is what you need to know about Option Thinking:

1) Always consider at least 3-7 options before making a change. Avoid immediately going to the tried-and-true option. You may end up there, but don't start there.

2) Find the 3 options in a counterintuitive way. Most people will start their thinking by looking at Worst Case Scenario (WCS) first. The logic is if you have that covered, you can only go up from there. I find that people who look at WCS first rarely will consider Best Case Scenario (BCS). Consequently, I propose that you always look at BCS first, WCS second and Most Probable Case Scenario (MPCS) third. This will ensure that you seek a wide enough array of Options. In the long run, the groups that seek the widest array of options make the best decisions because they have consciously or unconsciously considered more contingencies.

3) The reason to look at BCS first is not because you are likely to use it. BCS is used less than 1% of the time. So why bother? The answer is to stretch people's thought processes to consider something new and novel. It expands the option set and causes people to think more broadly about the issue. It also helps to raise general expectations. Make sure the first Option you consider stretches everyone's thinking, rather than attempting to solve the problem.

4) To be able to compare different views of a BCS on a level playing field, it is important to select good criteria to use to evaluate possible BCS's. That may help to level the playing field so apples will be compared to other apples and oranges to oranges.

5) Make sure to ask many questions and look at the issue from several points of view before you just start to generate Options. Often people think they understand the problem, but, when revisiting it from another point of view, different options immediately emerge. You can never ask enough questions.

6) Identify and question all of the assumptions you are making about the issue. Unwarranted assumptions often lead to foregone conclusions. The things that we take for granted often mask underlying issues. Maybe it has been a while since you have taken a good hard look and reality tested some of your beliefs about the way in which you conduct yourself.

7) It is best to attempt to solve the most reasonable statement of the problem. Many times problems appear in an inarticulate form. It may be very late in the problem process. It may seek to address issues totally out of your control. Make sure you can get your hands around the problem. Make sure that you are not just putting a Band-Aid on a symptom of another deeper problem.

8) Know several methods to get "unstuck." Option thinkers never run out of ideas. There are many ways to learn to think differently. Sometimes, it is our thought process that is as much of an issue as the problem itself.

ACTION

Change can be a gradual process. Often we do not move directly from black to white. We stop and spend some time in gray figuring out next steps. The key issue is to overcome the inertia and "analysis paralysis" that stops us from taking that ever important first leap of faith into the abyss of our future. Taking the wrong first step (assuming that it is not fatal) is preferable to not taking a step at all.

When making changes, it is important to start off with the "lowest hanging fruit." Do the things that seem easiest. Fear of Failure may still be lurking in the background. The more success that you have during initial stages of action, the more likely you will be to stay on track.

Remember that it takes 21-30 days for new behaviors to become habits, so one action will not be enough. It will be important to stay on track. Relapses into old behaviors may occur during this period. That is natural and normal and should be viewed as par for the course.

When Fear of Failure is allowed to creep in again, you may be tempted to abandon the behavior change entirely. Stay Strong. The real benefits of the change may not be apparent for a while. In the long run, the more changes you make successfully, the more confidence you will feel about being able to handle almost any change that comes your way.

The people who thrive on change look forward to it because they minimize the time they spend in denial and anger. They quickly jump into Option Thinking and Action when change is required. They realize that people, organizations and technology are dynamic and flexible. They view every change as an opportunity to increase their options. They have a great track record in being able to transform themselves when necessary.

A brief word about Chaos Theory is in order. Theorists use the word CHAORDER (a combination of the words chaos and order) to describe a very interesting phenomenon. Few things, in and of themselves, are either chaotic or orderly. It is often a function of the vantage point of the observer that determines this.

If you are moving faster than the changes happening around you, then change seems orderly and quite predictable. If, on the other hand, you are moving more slowly than the changes around you, then changes will seem random and chaotic.

In other words, it doesn't matter so much how fast the world is changing, it only matters how fast you are moving in relation to it.

So how fast are you moving?

THOUGHT BOMBS TO PONDER:

1) Do you like change? Do you love change? Do you like chaos? What is your first reaction to the need for change?
2) How much time do you spend in denial or getting angry about changes that you have to make?
3) Do you practice making small changes every day? Do you look forward to trying out new ways of behavior?
4) How many options do you consider when you need to make changes? Can you come up with at least 3 options for each change?
5) Do you thrive on change? Would you be happier and more successful if you embraced changes more readily?

CHAPTER 22

MOVING UP THE CORPORATE LADDER

COMMON SENSE

If you want to get promoted, work hard. Do what is asked of you. Keep your nose to the grindstone, and you will be rewarded when a position opens up.

UNCOMMON SENSE

Being promoted involves changing your behavior and focus once you reach a certain level of the organization. You are more likely to get promoted when you demonstrate finesse and a higher than average level of understanding of corporate politics.

One of the goals that many middle managers aspire to is reaching the lofty perches held by Senior Management. This transition is unlike any other transition that you have ever experienced. Guidelines for effectively making this transition have rarely been described. Training programs rarely deal with the subtleties involved.

Until now. If you are nearing this transition, pay close attention.

In many organizations, this transition occurs at the Director/Junior Vice President level. You have worked your entire career to get to this point, and you feel that all of your past learning and experiences are all that you need to make this hurdle. WRONG. This transition is not just about moving up to another level. You will need an almost entirely different set of criteria in order to be successful.

Consider the illustration below:

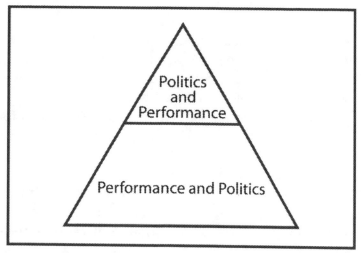

Diagram 5

Moving from anywhere in the lower levels of the organization up to the line that divides the triangle into 2 segments involves focusing upon PERFORMANCE first and POLITICS second. You will be judged largely upon your ability to "get it done."

Performance is definitely valued over finesse, grace and/or politic. You might have learned to step over, around or through other employees in order to attain maximum performance levels. You may have seen others be rude, discourteous, insensitive and overly ambitious in their efforts to outshine the competition. Knowledge is viewed as power, and employees regularly guard and withhold what they know from others. No effort to blame others is spared, and rumors and gossip abound.

Competition can be fierce with lots of infighting and possibly even throwing their compatriots "under the bus" to avoid blame. Gladiator battles often take place where employees are pitted against one another to determine the best performers. Elbows are thrown and "all is fair in love and war" becomes the motto. This occurs because there are fewer positions at the top, and the organization often engages in its own unique survival of the fittest contests. People rationalize "bad behavior" by thinking that they have to do whatever is necessary to make it to the top.

The sad part is that these rough and tumble methods become ingrained in everyone, and this behavior is viewed as "normal." If you have risen quickly through the organization, you may believe that this aggressive style is a valuable asset as you climb higher and higher on the corporate ladder. You also might be in for a big surprise.

Once you cross that imaginary line, the criteria you employ for your continued success must change in a dramatic fashion. The sad part is that no one tells you that they change. You are just supposed to know that you will now be judged by your POLITIC first and your PERFORMANCE second.

When I use the term politic, I again refer to your ability to position your ideas and strategies in front of your peers and Senior Management so that they can be received in the most optimal fashion while being truthful and honest. The loudest voice no longer wins. Speaking first may also not be desirable. Knowing which way the wind is blowing matters. Reading the trends and body language of others will help you to know whether to "hold 'em, fold 'em or return another day."

Take the case of Irv, an engineer with a Master's degree in Electrical Engineering from a prestigious university. He had worked for small start-up and large mature companies and was quite experienced in his field. He knew his stuff cold.

Unfortunately Irv had never attended "Charm School for Bright Technical People." Irv's issue was that few people were willing to work with him. Anyone assigned to a project with him once rarely accepted/desired a second opportunity to work with him.

In his own words, Irv focused on the "truth." Of course, Irv's truth and the truth of others often were different, but Irv was insistent that his truth had a capital "T." He didn't pay much attention to the way in which he presented it. In his words, "I don't have time to sugar coat things. We've got schedules to meet. So I just tell it like it is." As long as he believed that his view was correct, Irv dug his heels in and defended his thoughts to the bitter end. No concessions. No surrender.

Additionally, he:

1) Mocked and taunted anyone who disagreed with him
2) Grandstanded and showcased his experience, while denigrating the experience of others
3) Interrupted, ambushed and attacked anyone who did not fully accept his ideas (Irv operated with the "all or nothing" principle. It didn't matter to Irv if the person who questioned him was a subordinate, colleague, boss, member of Senior Management or customer.)
4) Constantly defended his behavior by saying he was only interested in the "Truth." He defiantly pointed out that he "didn't suffer idiots well."

Irv had reached the level of Associate Director and was looking for another promotion. He was surprised and amazed when he was repeatedly bypassed and eclipsed by less talented "butt kissers" (another of Irv's favorite terms).

What Irv did not want to realize was that the criteria for further promotion to the Director level had changed. It involved focus on well-developed political and interpersonal skills, rather than on straightforward performance.

Irv did not want to understand or accept that the way in which he presented his data mattered. He could not understand that his unwillingness to solve conflicts in a more subtle manner was detrimental. Irv thought that the faster he solved the conflict, the better. He rarely considered how others felt in the midst of conflict. As long as the issue got resolved, he couldn't understand why his peers were so "sensitive." Playing well with others was an undeveloped skill for him.

Irv was an ideal candidate for "Charm School for Bright Technical People," a program I developed after more than 30 years of working with scientists, engineers and financial analysts. Some of the topics covered include learning how to:

1) Present ideas so that they have the maximum opportunity to be favorably received
2) Tailor your message/sales call for each listener
3) Listen in order to understand instead of to respond
4) Disagree softly, keeping your focus on finding "common ground"
5) CAREfront others with empathy and support for the person, thereby separating issues with the person from the problem at hand
6) Say "No" to another person's idea without destroying their creativity or their willingness to offer more ideas in the future
7) Develop trust and high credibility with coworkers and customers.

(Note: For more complete information on this program, please see my website at www.drtomentertrainer.com.)

When I mentioned these ideas to Irv, he said that he possessed all of those skills. He claimed that he knew how to behave in a more appropriate manner. When I asked him why he wasn't using his "alleged" skills, his responses included:

1) I don't have the time to do that. I am working on too many different projects. I would be delayed if I had to think about each interaction and plan accordingly.
2) I don't want to appear to be disingenuous (Irv thought of these skills as phony and he prided himself on "being real" at all times).
3) The straight truth is more important in the long run.
4) It takes too long.
5) I get easily frustrated when I deal with incompetent or dishonest people.

I couldn't resist telling Irv that he was "too smart to be behaving so stupidly." He kept thinking about winning each battle, but he was certainly losing many of the wars that he was involved in.

His desire for promotion was moot until he was willing to see the light. What Irv saw as the "short cut" was proving to be the "long cut." Knowing what to do and then deciding not to do it was not helping him in the short or the long run. He was quickly wearing out his welcome at this company (as he had done in previous companies) and was destined for either another premature exit or a mid-level staff position where he reported to only 1 person.

It was not likely that he would be asked to ever present at an open meeting. He would not receive the exposure to Senior Management that was necessary for him to be considered for the position of Director.

Knowing what to do and how to handle yourself is a whopping 10% of the battle. Being sensitive to delicate situations and conscientiously deciding to change your behavior is the next 30% of the battle. Changing your behavior is 60% of the battle. The proof of your knowledge and good intentions is your new behavioral skill set and the impact that you make. Having good intentions without having corresponding good impact is not enough.

After months of work with Irv, I still am not entirely optimistic that Irv will see the light and change his behavior. I suspect that some of Irv's reluctance to change his behavior is rooted in "old scripts" that have been with him for his entire career. Irv's self-concept is tightly wrapped around his need to be right. That seems more important to him at work AND at home than career or relationship enhancement.

All of his great years of experience may be for naught if he doesn't take a good hard look at himself and decide how he wants to finish his career. In his mid-fifties, Irv may choose to preserve his image of himself. That is significantly easier than owning up to his marital and career choices.

In cases like Irv, it often takes a major trauma (e.g., getting fired, going through a divorce) before a person is willing to do the introspection and self CAREfrontation necessary to change behaviors. I have seen too many bright and talented people top out too early in their careers and then spend the rest of their wondering why "everyone out there was against me."

THOUGHT BOMBS TO PONDER

1) Are you like Irv? Is being "right" more important than the significant work and home relationships that you have?
2) What is more important to you? Performance? Politics? The subtle mixture of performance and politics?
3) Do you have AND use all of the Charm School skills on a regular basis? Remember these skills are not innate. They can all be learned and mastered by engaging the right models and mentors. The choice is up to you.
4) How well do you play with others? How sensitive are you to "pulse" of the group? Do you know when "to hold 'em and when to fold 'em?
5) Have you discussed the necessity for these political skills with your boss and other members of Senior Management?

CHAPTER 23

FORCE IS NOT ALWAYS THE BEST ANSWER

COMMON SENSE

There are times when rules have to be followed. Rules may be written down or just assumed, but sometimes there just isn't enough time or necessity to be able to sit down and explain everything to everyone. Know what the rules are and enforce them consistently.

UNCOMMON SENSE

Rules were written at a point in time to deal with certain problems and issues. They were written with certain situations in mind to give structure and clear guidance to individuals. However, there are times when you should use your own discretion in handling difficult situations.

Rules are rules. They were created for good reasons. Many rules are written to correct previous indiscretions. They provide a solid foundation for an employee to know what will be expected. However, there are times when UnCommon Sense dictates handling unique situations in a unique manner.

In the correctional setting, there are often adversarial relationships between offenders and correctional officers. Reasons for this are too numerous to mention, but at times this contentious relationship can become heated and create a flashpoint. It becomes particularly difficult when both offender and correctional officer believe something "isn't quite right."

Prisoners are assessed and then typically categorized as Level 1-Level 4 as a function of the offense they committed, their behavior in prison and other potential risk factors. Level 1 offenders are given opportunities to leave their cell to interact with other offenders, while Level 4 offenders are often restricted to their cell. That means they are also served food in their cell. At mealtime, a tray is passed into the cell and then it must be passed back out after the meal is eaten. The reason is simple. The tray could be used or modified to become a weapon. Therefore for safety and security reasons, the tray must be returned after each meal. Periodically, an offender will refuse to return a tray. This is a clear violation of prison protocol and can result in further disciplinary action. The immediate issue though is the return of the tray.

Correctional officers have a carefully scripted set of instructions that they must follow in order to retrieve the tray. They must ask for the tray several times, clearly stating the consequences for noncompliance. They must tell the offender that non-compliance will be met by having the offender "extracted" from the cell in order to retrieve the tray. Extraction teams are trained to deal with this situation in a manner to minimize any potential physical harm to the offender and other correctional officers.

A team of individuals will typically suit up in riot gear. They will videotape the extraction to provide evidence that only necessary force was used in the extraction. They will tell the offender that they will use a pepper spray like substance, if necessary. The team will ask one final time for the tray and then enter the cell, if the tray is not given back. Not a pleasant scene for anyone.

In one correctional setting, a Level 4 offender affectionately nick named "Manster" (Half Man, Half Monster), was regularly extracted from his cell monthly for some kind of rule violation. Manster was African-American. The offender on his left was affiliated with Nazi low riders. The offender on his right was a member of a Southern Mexican gang. The entire floor was comprised of violent and difficult offenders.

Manster always had something to complain about (e.g., he wasn't getting as much food as others; his food wasn't hot; he felt disrespected by several of the correctional officers). Most of the correctional officers had heard these complaints often enough and did not take them seriously. They did not investigate the claims and simply wrote them off as Manster wanting to get out of his cell. They figured that he liked the challenge of seeing how many officers it would take and how long it would take for the correctional officers to extract him. It seemed like a monthly game. When they used the pepper spray on him, Manster opened up his mouth to show that it didn't affect him. He claimed that he liked it.

One day, the ombudsman for the facility, Mr. K. was on site. Mr. K. was also African-American. He had spoken to Manster several times before and knew about his volatile blow ups. On this day, Manster had flooded his cell by stopping up the toilet, placed his bedding over the door and put human waste on the door as well. He was furious in his cell screaming about his food again. The captain who headed the extraction team told Mr. K that the team was gearing up to extract Manster again. Mr. K. asked if he might be able to talk with Manster prior to the use of the extraction team. The captain thought it was a waste of time but reluctantly agreed.

Mr. K. went to Manster's cell and asked Manster if he wanted to talk to him. Manster proceeded to complain that none of the correctional officers were willing to listen to him about what was happening to his food. Manster asked, "Where is the $#@%^ extraction team?" Mr. K. said that they were standing by ready to extract him. Then Mr. K. said, "Manster, I am here and willing to talk with you if you want, but you will have to do a few things for me first."

"Like what?" Mr. K said, "First, I need you to stop flushing the toilet in your cell. I also need you to take your bedding away from the door, and I need you to clean the waste from the door because it smells bad. If you do those things for me, I am willing to listen to you."

Because Mr. K. had demonstrated that he had been willing to listen in the past, Manster agreed to do as requested. He then proceeded to tell the following story.

He said, "Mr. K., they're messing with my food here. Every time Corrrectional Officers A and B are delivering food, they do bad things. They show me my food and then dump it onto the floor in front of my cell. Then they scoop it up and put it back on my tray. Then they give it to me. That's wrong. No one deserves to be treated that way. I swear that they do it when no one else is around."

Mr. K. asked, "Do they do that with others' food as well?"

Manster said he thought so. Mr. K. said he would look into it and asked Manster to give him his tray. Manster agreed without having to be extracted from his cell.

Mr. K. first checked with the Captain in charge of that unit. He explained what Manster had said and the Captain denied that anything like that was going on. He said he had personally watched those 2 Correctional Officers deliver food and that they always did it in the correct manner.

Mr. K went to check with the offenders on either side of Manster's cell. When Mr. K asked the Nazi low rider about whether his food had been tampered with, he received a mixed reply. Because offenders are extremely concerned about the perceptions that their cell neighbors have of them, he yelled racial epithets at Mr. K. and denied that there was a problem. Meanwhile, he stepped back further into his cell, where no one could see him, and started to nod his head up and down confirming Manster's story.

The exact same response was received from the Southern Mexican gang member. Mr. K. decided to go to captain and ask that a surveillance camera be installed so that the Correctional Officers behavior could be viewed when no one else was around. The captain thought it was a waste of time.

However, within a week after the camera was installed, Correctional Officers A and B were videotaped doing exactly what Manster had claimed. They were each disciplined and moved to other facilities.

The upshot of this example is that almost one year later, one of these staff members was assaulted in another facility by another inmate with a knife. While he was stabbing the Correctional officer, he whispered to him, "This is for Manster."

The critical element is that a violent cell extraction was avoided because Mr. K. was willing to listen to an offender whom no one else would listen to. Clearly, Manster had many issues and complaints, but this time his issue was real.

Employees who work in customer service or support groups hear so many complaints and gripes that they often are quick to discount the veracity of many of the claims that they here. They tend to "go by the book" in that situation. Every once in a while, listening to understand what the other person is saying opens up the door for a better solution.

THOUGHT BOMBS TO PONDER:

1) Do you enforce all of the rules that are part of your job? Do you feel that "rules are rules" and are meant to be followed all of the time?
2) Are there times when you can see alternative approaches to difficult problems that might work better than the "rules"? How do you feel when you think about not following the "rules"?
3) When you have heard the same type of complaints over and over, do you still listen carefully, in case this particular situation might be unique?
4) Are you more likely to ask for "permission" or for "forgiveness"?
5) What is more important to you: following the rules or doing the right thing (when they potentially conflict)?

CHAPTER 24

MORTGAGE OR INTEGRITY

COMMON SENSE

When you choose to work for an organization, you are obligated to do what you are asked to do. You may not always like it or understand it. You should trust the judgment of Senior Management, since they may have more information than you do about a specific situation. You should not do things that are illegal.

UNCOMMON SENSE

Recent studies have shown that more than 70% of leaders are asked to do something "questionable" during the course of their career. The activity may not be illegal or immoral, but it may be perceived as "not right" by the leader. While you owe loyalty to your organization, you also owe loyalty to the man/woman in the mirror. Ultimately, you must be able to justify to yourself what you do.

There are times when leaders need to make tough choices. Those choices can involve getting paid, keeping your job or doing the right thing. I am happy to say that, although I have been fired more times than I care to admit (usually for doing what I thought was the right thing as opposed to being incompetent), I sleep well at night knowing that I have behaved in an honorable manner. A critical example comes to mind.

A colleague and I were hired by a correctional medical facility to present a program on team building to the nursing staff. We were delighted to accept the offer, believing that we could help all parties involved. We asked to speak with Senior Staff members so that we could get an accurate picture of the relevant issues.

We first spoke with the senior person, the Director of Nursing. Her comments gave us the feeling that it would be helpful for us to check in with her staff. Their comments gave us the feeling that we ought to put "boots on the ground" and speak directly with RN's and LVN's who worked in the system. We created an opportunity for staff members to speak to us confidentially, if they wanted to.

It was as if we had opened up the floodgates because we heard from more than half of the staff. They expressed their appreciation for our offer to listen. Although we weren't seeking to uncover information about unsafe working conditions or safety and security violations, that is exactly what we heard. Some of them were truly of concern. We felt that it would be hard for us to conduct a training program on teambuilding when legitimate concerns about safety and security were not being addressed.

Several examples of their concerns were:

1) Nurses who worked on the 3rd shift were supposed to give medications to offenders in the middle of the night. These nurses were supposed to be escorted by correctional officers as they made their rounds. Unfortunately, some of the correctional officers on duty during this time period were asleep. Numerous complaints to correctional captains were made, but no changes occurred. The nurses, in violation of policy and at great personal risk to themselves, often made the rounds anyway and passed out medications (some of which included strong narcotics) unaccompanied.

2) Hazardous waste, including needles used to inject medications, were supposed to be picked up daily from disposal bins. This was critical because these disposal bins were located in places where offenders had potential access to them. Syringes could be used as weapons if they found their way into offender's hands. Several individuals reported that these disposal bins were often picked up weekly or even worse every two weeks.

3) Nurses were supposed to wear vests to protect themselves from potential attack. The vests that were available for

part-time nurses or replacement nurses were so dirty and smelled so bad that many of the nurses chose to do their rounds without them. Numerous complaints to clean the vests were made, but no action was taken.

We asked ourselves the "mortgage vs. integrity" question. Should we report what we had found, despite the fact that it was outside the scope of work that we were hired to do? Or should we simply do as we were told and conduct the teambuilding program. My mortgage needed to be paid, but not at the price of our conscience.

Instead of going to the local newspaper with our findings or seeking to glorify ourselves as "whistle blowers," we discretely went to the Senior Management team of the facility and offered to prepare a confidential report concerning what we had been told by staff. We offered to do this without asking for additional remuneration, believing that it was the right thing to do. We even proposed options to address many of the issues raised quickly and effectively. We argued that this gesture would show the nursing team that their concerns were being heard and acted upon. We felt that it would provide a good kick start for the teambuilding program.

Doing the right thing has consequences at times. The expression of "no good deed goes unpunished" is particularly meaningful here. We were told to stick to the scope of our contract. We were asked why we had gone looking for violations. We reported that we hadn't but that the violations were pointed out to us because we were willing to listen to staff. The management team did not see the connection between dealing with the complaints and delivering the team building program.

The bad news was that we were relieved of our responsibilities within a short period of time. The good news was that the violations were eventually addressed.

Standing tall is what leaders do even when it is not popular. Colleagues of mine have argued that it is easier to stand tall when you are a consultant. You are not vested in the long-term success of the organization. You simply find another place to work. They argue that long-term employees of organizations have a lot more at stake including pensions and other life-long benefits.

I honor their views, but it is hard to assign a value to being able to look at the man/woman in the mirror, knowing that you have done the right thing.

THOUGHT BOMBS TO PONDER

1) Have you ever been placed into a situation where you were asked to "look the other way?" What did you do? How did you feel?
2) When you discovered a situation that didn't feel "quite right" to you, what did you do? Was your discovery valued by your organization?
3) How important is respecting the man/woman in the mirror vs. keeping your job? In a previous chapter, I suggested that Rule # 1 was to keep your job and Rule # 2 was to remember Rule # 1. How do you feel?
4) Can you put a price tag on your integrity? What is that price?
5) What advice would you have offered me if I came to you to discuss the situation described in this chapter?

CHAPTER 25

THE NORMALIZATION OF DEVIANCE

COMMON SENSE

When you see a problem, speak up about it. However, after you have spoken up about it, it is up to Senior Management to decide what action to take.

UNCOMMON SENSE

With due respect to Senior Management, leaders must stand tall when they truly believe there is a problem. This is particularly true when human lives lie in the balance.

I was a presenter at a program where I had the great honor of following a NASA astronaut to the stage. His presentation was moving and thought provoking as he described his experiences at NASA prior to his trip into space. NASA is one of the most revered organizations in the public sector. It usually receives high marks from NASA employees and from the public. However, even the best organizations can experience difficulties.

The astronaut described a phenomenon that occurred at NASA, one that occurs daily at numerous organizations in both the public and private sector. He spoke with reverence about NASA but appealed to the audience to consider what their reaction might have been if the event he described had happened within their organization. This example is in no way intended as an indictment of NASA. It represents an issue that must be surfaced and dealt with by many leaders in many organizations.

The astronaut began to describe what was happening as NASA prepared for the ill-fated launch of the Challenger in 1986. As they were preparing for the launch, there was difficulty with the O Rings.

During the first 25 tests of the O Rings, a malfunction occurred more than 15 times. This should have caused concern for all involved.

The astronaut asked the audience what they would have done, had they been astronauts in the program awaiting their turn to rocket into space. While no one wanted to head into space with questionable equipment, no one wanted to raise questions either. Many astronauts assumed that, since the problem was evident, engineers were working to solve the problem. Other astronauts admitted that they were reluctant to speak up for fear that they might lose the opportunity to go into space. After all, if you had spent your entire life preparing to fly on a mission into outer space, would you have risked that opportunity by questioning mission control? The astronauts essentially turned a blind eye to the problem.

What about the engineers? I have worked with engineers for many years. I love engineers. They are truth tellers to the nth degree. While I sometimes have to offer to rent them a personality so that they know what it is like to have one, I know I can count on them to tell the truth in almost every situation. Sometimes they will tell the truth without regard for personal or organizational consequences. They are hard wired to do so. The engineers spoke up many times to anyone that would listen. They had serious concerns about the O Rings.

However, the mission was late and already over budget. There was huge political pressure to get the launch under way. Staff members at NASA were optimistic that they would be able to solve the problem and that the launch would go off as scheduled. In retrospect, a delay would have been advisable.

The correct functioning of the O Ring was vital for the launch of the Challenger orbiter. The O Ring failure that occurred following the launch caused a breach that allowed pressurized hot gas from within the solid rocket motor to reach the outside. This in turn impinged upon the adjacent hardware and external fuel tank. This led to the separation and structural failure of the external fuel tank. Once this occurred, aerodynamic forces destroyed the Challenger Orbiter

73 seconds into the flight over the Atlantic Ocean, instantly killing everyone on board.

The astronaut identified a phrase to describe what had occurred at NASA. He described the phenomenon as a "normalization of deviance." He suggested that the fact that the O Ring was tested 25 times and NOT REDESIGNED was not the critical issue. He suggested that, at a world class organization such as NASA, where astronauts put their lives on the line, the O Ring should have been reviewed and redesigned after the FIRST failure.

After all of the failed attempts, what was considered "out of the ordinary" or at worst "deviant" became the new normal. Everyone just accepted the fact that the O Rings had malfunctioned.

Too often organizations overlook problems until something problematic occurs. When queried, employees within the organization offer numerous rationalizations that seem to make sense until a problem arises. I have heard all of the following reasons numerous times:

1) I'm not the only one who saw it. Why is it my responsibility to say something?
2) That is for Senior Management to decide. That is why they get paid the big bucks.
3) There are lots of issues bigger than that around here and no one seems to deal with those either.
4) I don't want to rock the boat.
5) This company doesn't like whiners. I just mind my own business and keep doing my job.
6) I said something once, and I got into trouble. I am keeping my mouth shut.
7) I knew someone who spoke up as a "whistle blower." He got fired. I need this job.

Many classic studies describe the series of decisions that employees must make BEFORE they are likely to take action. The kinds of questions they ask include:

1) Is it an emergency?
2) Am I the only one that sees this as an emergency?
3) Is it my responsibility to deal with this emergency?
4) Am I competent to deal with this emergency?
5) Are there negative consequences to dealing with this emergency, if I make a mistake?
6) How hard would it be to deal with this emergency?

The easiest way to deal with a difficult situation is to perceive the situation as not being an emergency. No further self-reflection is required. When you see an individual lying on the sidewalk, most of us will quickly assume that the individual is drunk or homeless by choice or running a scam. That makes it easy for us to walk away. Think of the easy rationalizations that come to your mind when faced with equivalent situations.

Dante and more recently Martin Luther King Jr. both have suggested that "the hottest places in hell are reserved for those who, in times of great moral crisis, maintain their neutrality. When these situations occur in the workplace, they are not viewed as a "moral crisis." Should they be viewed that way?

THOUGHT BOMBS TO PONDER:

1) How likely are you to stand up and identify significant errors in your organization?
2) How receptive is your organization to leaders who identify such errors?
3) How often have you rationalized/justified not doing anything in a situation where you feel that "something should be done?"
4) Are there practices in your organization that are not acceptable, but have been "normalized" because no one has pointed them out?
5) How would you feel if a "normalized" practice resulted in the death or injury to someone that you worked with?

CHAPTER 26

PROACTIVITY IS NOT ALWAYS THE BEST SOLUTION

COMMON SENSE

When a problem arises, it is important to deal with it promptly so that it doesn't become bigger and more difficult to solve. Managers are usually good at dealing with problems quickly because they recognize the potential impact on productivity. Leaders also deal with problems but in a different manner. They are more likely to use them to grow their staff and solve the problem simultaneously.

UNCOMMON SENSE

Throughout this this entire book, you have been encouraged to take a proactive stance. Most of the time that works well. Like any guideline, there are exceptions. At times, dealing with a situation more patiently can have equal or better results.

In this book, I have suggested that you take an active, forward-looking stance when dealing with problems. It demonstrates your confidence, courage and conviction to be willing to deal with issues directly. You develop the belief that problems can be turned into opportunities. However, this is not always the case.

Union-Management negotiations are not always open and honest. At times, they can be quite contentious. The negotiations can be stalled over what seems to be small/trivial issues like small wage increases in hourly pay. One good rule of thumb to attend to is that, when groups argue over small issues, it usually is an indicator that there are big "elephant in the room" issues underlying these small issues.

Often these small issues are raised for a variety of reasons such as:

1) Payback for bad faith in prior negotiations
2) Feelings of unilateral or mutual disrespect
3) Only one side had to make concessions during the last round of negotiations
4) Personal animosity between negotiation sides
5) A lack of consideration between the parties

Almost all of these underlying issues were present during a particularly nasty negotiation at an airline. The most contentious issue was a raise of 30 cents per hour. Both sides were adamant about their positions, and there was talk of a strike if the issue was not settled.

Shortly after the impasse was reached, vandalism began to occur on aircraft. The vandalism consisted of anti-company graffiti being scrawled on plastic and/or glass in the restrooms of the planes. This was embarrassing to the company and quite visible to customers.

Each episode of vandalism cost the company approximately $150 to repair. It also potentially delayed flights if the graffiti was spotted just before departure. There had been 8 episodes of this vandalism when I received a call from the VP of Human Resources, who asked for suggestions to stop the vandalism.

The CEO of the airline was a hard liner who was livid that such acts were occurring. It was determined that the potential culprits of the vandalism were members of one group of maintenance employees consisting of about 45 employees at one particular location where aircraft received regular servicing. Of these 45 employees, a core of 10 vocal employees was considered the most likely perpetrators of these actions.

The CEO was bent on demanding that each employee in this group undergo questioning using a polygraph to determine the veracity of their answers. Another option that the CEO favored was the installation of hidden cameras in the aircraft designed to catch the perpetrators in action. This would have been quite costly. An additional problem was how to install such cameras without the maintenance staff being aware of their presence. Since the cameras would have to be placed in the bathrooms, it opened up another more serious issue concerning privacy issues for employees and customers.

The VP of Human Resources begged the CEO to show restraint, while he sought other options, so as not to inflame the already difficult contract negotiations.

When I went to discuss the issue with the VP, I had prepared several options for him to consider including:

1) Holding meetings with union employees that allowed for the venting of strong feelings involved in the negotiations. The idea was that if employees felt that they were being listened to, they might have less need to vandalize the aircraft.
2) Giving employees the opportunity to vent their feelings through an anonymous questionnaire. The logic here was similar to the first suggestion.
3) Offering a small concession on the wage issue or any other negotiation issue as a show of good faith.
4) Having members of the management team visit various sites and conduct LBWA visits to show their care, compassion and concern for employees
5) Offering a small amount of money for each day that no vandalism occurred that would be used for a party for all maintenance employees to show corporate appreciation for halting the vandalism.

I am experienced in dealing with angry feelings and have offered numerous facilitations to give people an opportunity to vent. I was fully prepared to meet with angry union members so that cooler heads could potentially prevail. I was personally leaning toward that option, strongly believing that the union members just wanted an opportunity to be heard. I felt that the vandalism was the result of their frustration at not being able to speak directly to the Senior Management team.

I stressed the urgency of being proactive and dealing directly with the group of employees who were alleged to be involved in the vandalism. The cost for repair was not as much of an issue as the embarrassment it caused when the graffiti was seen by the public. The CEO was angry because he felt that the union was just "trying to show him up."

The VP of Human Resources listened to the options carefully and then suggested that he would "run them up the flagpole" with other members of Senior Management before suggesting them to the CEO. He wanted to be sure that there would be strong support for at least one of the options so that he would not have to present them to the CEO alone. He took about a week to consult with his peers. During this time, 4 more episodes of vandalism occurred, which were all found and repaired before the aircraft were put into service.

I had a second meeting with the VP and again stressed the urgency for a strong, proactive response. Since support from his peers was tepid at best, the VP kept searching for options that might be more palatable to the CEO. It was clear that he was equally concerned with appeasing the CEO as he was dealing with the disgruntled union members.

His reluctance to present other ideas to the CEO lasted for almost a month. I had expected that the acts of vandalism would increase during this time frame. However, during that month there were only 2 more episodes of vandalism. There were a total of 14 episodes and a total repair cost of under $2500 (far less than the cost of any of the proposed interventions I suggested.)

The negotiations were concluded within the next 3 months and business went on as usual. Although the CEO had wanted to "find and fire" the vandals, he was persuaded to let it go. I was not involved with the airline for the next round of negotiations 3 years later, but I assume that contentious issues came to the forefront again.

THOUGHT BOMBS TO PONDER

1) How quick are you to respond to problematic issues? Are you proactive most of the time?
2) How do you view problems? Reactively? Proactively?
3) Do you have the patience, interest and ability to use problems to grow your staff?
4) Do you react to the problem as stated, or do you look beneath the surface for underlying issues?
5) How do you feel when problems are not solved right away?
6) Have you ever struggled to find solutions to a problem only to find that it took care of itself?

CHAPTER 27

ARE YOU READY?

Congratulations! You have spent time, money and effort to read this book and get this far. I hope you feel excited. I hope you remember that 10% of the battle is learning what to do, that 30% is making the decision to move into action, and that 60% is about doing what you have decided.

You are 10% of the way there. In order to help you succeed, here are some more helpful thought bombs to consider.

THOUGHT BOMBS TO PONDER

1) Who are you as a leader today? What skills do you possess? What areas do you feel you could strengthen? Consider that we have talked about skill sets in:
   a) Motivation
   b) Communication
   c) Sales
   d) Customer Service
   e) Leadership
   f) Change
2) What is your strongest suit? How can you use what you do best to help strengthen other areas?
3) What kind of leader would you like to become? Describe what that leader can do. How is that leader viewed by people that surround him/her?
4) What is the first step that is easiest for you to attain? Remember to pick the low hanging fruit first. Who can help you? Support you? Give you feedback?
5) Are you ready? What are you waiting for? How will you hurdle the obstacles that may be in your path?

REVIEW

Let's review where we have been. Here are a few of the major themes that have been presented in this book:

EMOTIONS vs. LOGIC:

Every situation has both an emotional and logic element to it. Resist the temptation to jump right in and solve the logical part of the problem first without considering and dealing with the emotional element. Dealing with the emotional element first is much more likely to result in a collaborative relationship that will result in faster, more enduring logical options.

LISTEN FIRST, THEN SPEAK

The concept that leaders should speak first to demonstrate their leadership and vision is an antiquated notion. Today, the mark of a great leader is the ability to ask the right questions at the right time to the right people. Many examples were presented to show that calibrating the audience and truly listening to understand where people are coming from results in more respect and credibility for today's leader. Remember the Ask-Sell-Tell mantra. Showing humility and curiosity results in much more buy-in than just barking orders.

CAREFRONTATION vs. CONFRONTATION

Issues have to be dealt with. However, dealing with them by joining with others and then attacking the problem goes a long way. When you ask questions, show empathy, understanding and support, situations can be quickly diffused. When there is no perceived attack, there is less need for defensiveness. Remember, leaders are in it for the long haul. You may lose a battle or two, but you want to win the war.

THE 3 C's: CARE, COMPASSION AND CONCERN

Leaders go out of their way to develop relationships with individuals at every level of the organization. By creating "safe" environments, focusing on mutual goals and reaching out to everyone for input and help, leaders gain more buy in. This is not to suggest that leaders are "friends" with everyone. There are hard decisions that will have to be made, and they must be made from a "business" point of view. However, showing honest and genuine concern for others goes a long way. Leaders who are perceived as "real" are valued by everyone around them.

TRUST, CREDIBILITY AND RESPECT

Ultimately, everything you ever do as a leader is based on gaining and maintaining trust with others. Trust is the most precious commodity that a leader possesses. It can only be regained twice if it is lost. There are many intentional activities that leaders can engage in that build trust quickly.

Receiving frequent feedback from others about your trust and credibility allows you to manage those perceptions if they begin to drift in a negative manner. Earning respect and giving it in return keep relationships positive with high productivity. Nothing can help you be more productive and move faster than high trust, credibility and respect.

COMMUNICATE, COMMUNICATE, COMMUNICATE

Leaders who use emotionally evocative language and can get to the hearts of the people around them are more likely to be successful than leaders who just state facts. By using an economy of powerful language, leaders can share their vision, passion and excitement for the future. There is an element of "selling" involved in leadership. As long as you view "selling" as "helping others to achieve their goals," you should feel proud whenever you seek to "sell" your ideas.

DO THE RIGHT THING

Leaders are constantly checking with those around them: peers, staff, customers, stakeholders, the community, etc. However, at the end of the day, it is the woman/man in the mirror who matters the most. Leaders must be able to stand tall and feel proud of the decisions they make and the actions they have taken.

As Dr. Martin Luther King said, "The time is always right to do what is right." Too many leaders have succumbed to the temptations that accompany the power that they were granted. Don't become one of those people.

A FEW FINAL TIPS

START TODAY

There is no better time to get started than today. Remember you can't fix or change yesterday. You can only do something about today and tomorrow. Why not start on what could become the most fascinating part of your work journey and enhance your ability to lead? Look out your window. The world is waiting.

THERE ISN'T ONE BEST WAY TO DO ANYTHING

Your way is no better than my way. There is no one right way. Stop thinking my way or the highway. Lose those ideas.

You have learned a few things about Option Thinking. Seek at least 3 options before you just plow ahead. Leaders do not always find the path on their first try. Big deal. Just getting started and overcoming the inertia of "analysis paralysis" is a great first step.

TAKE THE FIRST STEP

Start with one thing. An easy thing. Something that you are fairly certain you can do. Do that. See how it feels. Ask others for feedback.

The only step that is really hard to take is the first one. Sometimes you need to leap before you look.

GET FEEDBACK

Feedback is the breakfast of champions. Solicit ideas and comments from those that you respect. Surround yourself with support. For some of you, it may be helpful to use a mentor, business or life coach to help you get started and to hold you accountable at various stages of your journey. There are many professionals available to help.

TELL PEOPLE WHAT YOU ARE DOING

One mistake that many leaders make when they change their behavior is to change without telling anyone around them. When you begin to behave differently and others do not understand why, they may have perceptions that are quite different than what you intend. Remember, it is about your impact, not your intentions.

Prepare others for the changes you are making by telling them what you are seeking to do and why you are seeking to do it. In this manner, they will have a better idea of your intentions, and hopefully those intentions will match their perceptions of your impact.

CREATE A "SAFE" ENVIRONMENT

By being open and honest about your actions, you are creating a learning environment where others can help you to accelerate your learning curve. You will make mistakes as you attempt new behaviors. That is par for the course. Don't abandon your attempts just because of a few missteps or relapses to previous behavior. In a "safe" environment, others can help you to get back on the right track. Focus should never be on blame, but on future, better options.

TRUST YOUR GUT

This process flows more smoothly when you use your internal barometer to determine what to do next. Some people get overly concerned about making mistakes. They attempt to do too much too quickly, or they move at a snail's pace.

Go at a pace that works for you. Check in with yourself often to see how you are feeling about your progress. Progress will not be linear; it will stop and start. It will plateau at times. Trust your own judgment as to the right pace and timing. The man/woman in the mirror is the most important judge that you will ever have to contend with.

FACE YOUR FEARS

Although the journey will be exciting and thrilling, it will also be pockmarked with fear. You have learned to deal with Fear of Failure. Face it directly. There is no way that you can become a great leader without facing, dealing with and reframing your attitude towards fear. It will be there. Be prepared. Be ready and overcome it.

THIS IS A JOURNEY

This book hopefully is a guide for the entire race. Remember that the race is a marathon, not a 100-yard dash. Journeys never end up going directly to where we expect or hope.

Simply having the courage to embark on the journey is a great first step. Where you end up—who knows? That is part of the sense of adventure that I hope you nurture as you progress. In the long run, it is so much more about the journey than about where you end up anyway.

HAVE FUN

It's party time now. That is the last thing I say every day when I go to work. I learned to do "party time" when I worked with dying and suicidal individuals. It was how I kept my spirits high when others around me were not in high spirits.

It is important that you bring a positive attitude as well as a smile with you 9 out of every 10 days.

If you had as much fun reading this book as I had writing it, then we both came to party. You might even buy my next book UnCommon Sense: Part Deux.

I always love to hear success stories, so let me know how you are progressing. I can be reached at DrTom4@aol.com.

In the meantime, LEAD THE WAY.

Dr. Tom Steiner
www.drtomtheentertrainer.com
www.drtomthecoach.com
The EnterTRAINer
October, 2016